# PUSH ME GENTLY, LORD

By

MARILYN MORAVEC
PAMELA HEIM
ROBERTA COLLINS

harvest publications
Arlington Heights, Illinois

Second Printing 1986

Copyright ©1985 by Harvest Publications
Printed in the United States of America
Library of Congress Catalog Number: 85-80100

Unless otherwise noted, Scripture references in Parts 1 and 2
are from the Holy Bible: New International Version. Copyright
©1978 by the International Bible Society. Used by permission
of Zondervan Bible Publishers; in Part 3, from The Amplified
Bible.

ISBN: 0-935797-21-1

Published by
Harvest Publications
Division of the Board of
Educational Ministries
Baptist General Conference
2002 S. Arlington Heights Rd.
Arlington Heights, Illinois 60005

# TABLE OF CONTENTS

# Preface

Women have been in the spotlight in recent years, both in secular and Christian circles. Many Christian women have modeled Christ's gracious spirit and led ministries at home, in the church and community and around the world. Yet some Christian women have retreated to quiet places, to the inconspicuous background, and often to ineffective isolation. They have deliberately sought inactive roles and given in to the ''your voice is not important'' implications which they hear in the more aggressive voices in the church and community.

Today, however, there is growing awareness not only of women's ability to minister, but of their responsibility as mature Christians. For example, at Chuck Swindoll's First Evangelical Free Church in Fullerton, Calif., Betty Coble, director of women's ministries, is bringing women together in dynamic ministry.

''The next five years will be explosive in women's ministries,'' predicts Betty.

Dr. Pamela Reeve, dean of women at Multnomah School

of the Bible, and seminar leader for women's ministries, sees as a direct outgrowth of Bible study groups a new impetus in ministry. She observes: "The past ten years have seen thousands of women involved in small group Bible studies. These in-depth studies have become the foundation for Christian maturity and for ministry. As women complete these courses, they ask, 'What do I do now?' "

The obvious "what next," says Dr. Reeve, is to minister to people and their needs. She concludes that, "The skills for ministry may be lacking, but the desire to reach out to people is a high priority among Christian women."

As we observe the church today, it is becoming apparent that more and more Christian women will seek opportunities for productive ministries as God leads them. In keeping with this new thrust in women's ministries, the burden of this book is to guide the Christian woman who wants to get involved. She may already be ministering but needs encouragement. She may see a need to minister, but does not know how to get started. Above all, she wants to follow biblical principles. And she wants to be the kind of successful person described in this book: "steadily becoming the unique person God intends her to become and...doing what He asks her to do."

In preparing this book, we've asked three prominent ministering women to offer a step-by-step process to help us become involved in serving others.

In Part 1, Marilyn Moravec, minister of adult education and counseling, makes it clear that to be prepared for ministry, we must have a growing relationship with God. "There is a way of being productive without being pushed, of carrying responsibilities without being strangled by them," writes Marilyn. She then shows us that relationships begin with ourselves, as Jesus commanded: "Love your neighbor as yourself." Our ministry to people is built on our relationships with them.

In Part 2, Pamela Heim, author and women's ministries speaker, provides models of ministry for various stages of life.

Examining the life of Moses, she helps us learn from his trials, failures and successes.

"The Lord has called every person to serve Him, and He has equipped each to minister uniquely in His church," writes Pamela. "We can sit on the sidelines and offer excuses for our lack of involvement in the work of the Kingdom. Or we can move into the action with confidence....He has sent us forth with His presence, with His name, with His power and with His gifts."

In Part 3, Roberta Collins, a pastor's wife and women's ministries speaker, gives us a formula for success: Knowing who you are + acting like who you are = success. "He won't throw you in over your head, beyond your ability, before your time," she assures us, writing from personal experience. God doesn't intend that we fail, but the problem is how to know when we succeed.

The beginning of ministry, says Roberta, is "committing yourself to intimately knowing Him."

In our world today there are needs so deep that we cannot treat them with band-aid solutions. But we can call upon God to minister through us to women who are abused, who are experiencing the pain of divorce, who are struggling in a tension-filled marriage, who are helping an aging parent, who are facing crippling disease, or who are making life-changing decisions.

God has an area in which He wants you to work. And He will guide you into being fully competent for that work. Can you accept the possibility of all you can be? This truly is the beginning of ministry.

# Facilitator's Guide

The following studies are designed for groups of not more than ten women who commit themselves for six consecutive sessions. The material may be used for smaller numbers and by as few as two who want to meet together for sharing. Regular meetings of an hour and a half should be scheduled weekly, biweekly or monthly. If possible, weekly meetings are ideal. The material also is useful for personal study or for retreats.

In group study, anyone who can show caring and acceptance can lead your discussions. If you are the facilitator, you must thoroughly work through each lesson in advance. It is important to realize that you are a member of the group, learning and growing yourself.

Group leader is not a teaching position. The word "facilitate" means "to make easier." Your most important function as facilitator will be to help create an atmosphere of openness, warmth and acceptance of one another. Such will assist the process of personal growth for each group member, as well as enhance your fellowship.

Your greatest asset as a facilitator is your life, your sharing and your love for other group members. For example, as facilitator, give the first answer when going around the group (as in Part I, Chapter 1, question 1). And be as self-disclosing as possible. This will set a pace of openness.

Some women in your group will not share too deeply. Do not call on them or push them in any way. For example, if in Part 1, Chapter 1, number 5, someone says she doesn't identify with any of the five women, simply acknowledge her response and go on to the next person. Not relating to a particular question or not sharing is acceptable. Silence does not necessarily indicate lack of interest. Trust God to be at work in each of you. You'll find acceptance is the soil for growth and change.

Some women who are in very hurting situations at this time in their lives may need more time to talk than the group session can provide. In this case, sensitively move the discussion along, and think of alternative ways the person's need can be met. For example, you or a group member may have coffee with her at another time. Your responsibility is to keep a balance between meeting individual needs and making sure each lesson is covered. You may need some real wisdom! Pray for this (James 1:5).

As you work through each lesson, have every section and all Scriptures read aloud by volunteers. Of course, the facilitator may read also. Do not call on anyone to read unless you know they won't mind. Some people have not returned to groups because they do not feel adequately able to read aloud.

Also, be sensitive to the fact that everyone is not skilled in finding their way around the Bible. In studying a Scripture passage, state where the book is and how to find it easily. For example, with a Proverbs reference you could say, "Right after Psalms, in about the middle of the Bible." For an Ephesians reference: "This is a small book after Corinthians in the New Testament." Finding Corinthians will be easier because of its size, so you reference Ephesians from there rather than from Galatians.

Most women will come prepared, but not all. Simply flex with that. Accept it and work with it. Encourage those who do not prepare the lesson to write their personal letters to God and do their journaling (more about this later) at home the next week. They will probably be more motivated then.

Contact absentees with a note or phone call. But accept the fact that not everyone will attend every week, although this is the ideal. Some women may drop out for personal reasons, or because they feel the material does not meet their needs. Accept this and do not take it personally; work heartily with those who come.

The first lesson in Part I can be done together without preparation in advance by participants. As facilitator, do your lesson ahead and then hand out the books at the first meeting, everyone working together at that time. Or you can hand out the books in advance. But this can be threatening to women who have never been in a small group before, or who are not familiar with the Scriptures. They feel overwhelmed by having to do a lesson on their own.

Do it one way or the other, i.e., do not give the books ahead of time to a few women. Either give the books to all participants (and then only if you feel certain they can complete the work alone), or do not give the books in advance at all.

Most questions in each lesson are designed for group discussion; a few are optional. Instructions immediately following will tell you how to handle the topic in group session. If "optional", give group members an opportunity to share. If no one offers, simply go on. Do not let this disturb you. God may be doing some deep and unspeakable works. Also, a few questions state clearly that they are for private use only. Skip them in group session and go on.

In Part I, most sessions end in group prayer. Do not go around the group praying in order. This puts pressure on each person to pray. Explain sentence praying, saying that it is simply talking to God in brief sentences; that He is there and you are conversing with Him as a group. Invite anyone to pray who would like to. Close the prayer time yourself or ask someone who you're certain will be comfortable praying.

The study questions for Part I are designed to be answered as you study the material together. For Parts II and III, it probably will work best to read the material first, then discuss the questions in your group.

Reread these instructions after you've led the first session. They will seem more understandable then. You'll be spending more time in this material than the other participants. We trust that God will use it powerfully in your personal life. He has done this for us as we have written it.

# PART I:
# SAYING ''YES, GOD''
# TO RELATIONSHIPS

By Marilyn Moravec

SECTION I: MY RELATIONSHIP WITH GOD

# 1
# *My #1 Personal Priority*

If you're like me, at times it seems as if life is getting out of control. It's not a good feeling: papers piling up around me, people wanting something from me, and the endless lists of responsibilities to fulfill.

It's at these times that I realize I've left the best of life and unwittingly chosen the treadmill. One thing age has taught me is that the treadmill style of living isn't worth it. It costs too much in terms of stress to my body, and it doesn't accomplish anything of deep value. The truth of I Corinthians 3—that the quality of my work will be tested—has sobered my viewpoint. It's made me realize that some works I think I *must* do are going to burn up before my eyes. They're "wood, hay and stubble." What I really want is to build what will last into eternity.

I also want to be free from feeling driven. I had known for a long time that this feeling is not really a result of having much to do, but of something deeper. I had sensed that there is a way of being productive without being pushed, of carrying responsibilities without being strangled by them. And now I've found that this is so! Though I still struggle to keep from feeling driven, there's been clear progress in my life, and I love it! I'm more relaxed and feeling more centered and anchored than ever before.

I'm writing this as a love gift to you, so that you can taste, with me, more and more of the abundant life Jesus came to give.

1.  Begin by reading Luke 10:38-42.

Martha sounds as if she is feeling the way I described myself earlier. Read the opening paragraph of this chapter again. Then recall a time when you shared Marilyn's and Martha's agitation, feeling "upset and worried about many things." When was it? How did it feel? (*Facilitator*: Go around your group giving your names and doing this exercise together. If anyone can't think of an example, she may just give her name.)

2.  Read Matthew 22:34-40 and Luke 10:25-41.

The *New Bible Commentary* suggests that both the parable of the Good Samaritan and the record of Jesus' conversation with Mary and Martha were recorded here by Luke to deepen our understanding of Jesus' summation of all the commandments. The practical love shown by the Samaritan and by Martha are secondary to the act of sitting at the Lord's feet listening to Him. Mary had learned to follow the "first and greatest commandment."[1]

3.  What do you think it means to "love the Lord your God with all your heart and with all your soul and with all your strength and with all your mind"? Specifically, what attitudes and what actions would you expect to see in someone obedient to this command? What would she be doing?

_____

_____

_____

4. Read the following descriptions (*Facilitator*: choose five different readers):

*Sharon* is 28, a mother of two toddlers. Daily she feels closed in. Sometimes it seems as if there is no place of refuge. She loves her husband and two little boys, but many days she secretly longs for a place of aloneness, of just being a person. Tonight her husband is at a church meeting and she feels resentful.

*Sandy* is 34 and divorced after 15 years of marriage. She and her three children live in a low-income apartment house near church. The children are active at church, but Sandy has found no friends in the congregation. She feels very unworthy as a Christian; this feeling often overwhelms her as she sits in a service, surrounded by what looks to her to be happy families. She longs to know that she is okay.

*Clare* is 67. Her husband Herb left her alone four years ago when he died suddenly of a heart attack. The adjustment to aloneness has been excruciating; 42 years of marriage have left her unprepared to cope with the realities of life alone. Her social security check is a day late and she finds herself feeling panicky.

*Karen* is a 36-year-old single, active in her church and enjoying her job. One night a week she practices with the choir, another night she helps with children's clubs, and a third night she bowls with the church league. Every other week she's in a Bible study with friends. Weekends are busy with social activities, chores and church. It's been two weeks since she's had an evening at home alone. She's beginning to feel exhausted and pressured.

*Sarah* is 47, with one married daughter and two children in college. For the first time in 24 years she is free. She knows she should be feeling great about this liberation; instead, she feels terrified. Every day is a new challenge to face life without demands. She feels a need for help, for direction.

5. Having heard these feelings and life situations, indicate which of the five women you feel you understand most. Feel free to

share the reason with your group and write it here (*Facilitator*: Go around the group, having each person share):

_____

_____

_____

6.   Although the feelings of our five friends are different, one word could describe them all: *AGITATION*. Each situation is painful and difficult in its own unique way. But in all we sense a lack of personal peace. Each woman needs a plan of action to deal with her life, which seems to some extent out of her control. Each has different unfulfilled needs. But for each, the plan of action must begin with the same first step: reordering priorities and centering life.

To think straight and to solve our life's problems, we each must begin at step 1. What do you think this is? Apply your answer especially to the woman you named in number 5.

_____

_____

_____

7.   Read again Luke 10:38-42. What was Martha feeling?

_____

_____

_____

How are her feelings similar to the feelings of the five women above?

_____

_____

_____

How did Martha and some of our five friends feel about the close people in their lives?

_____

_____

_____

8. What advice did Jesus give to Martha? Copy it directly from the Scripture. Then rewrite the same message in your own words.
Scripture:

_____

_____

_____

Your own words:

_____

_____

_____

9. What would you have felt if you had been Mary, and Martha was running around making the preparations? (I probably would have had a massive attack of the "guilts." How about you?)

_____

_____

_____

10. What kind of listener to Jesus would you be with all that activity going on around you? How do you think Mary managed to continue to listen to Jesus with Martha's fussing?

_____

_____

_____

11. Mary could quietly concentrate on Jesus with such racket and emotional turmoil going on around her for three reasons:
a) She was absolutely *convinced* that what she was doing was the most important pursuit of her life; listening to Jesus was her step #1 to all of life's agitations.
b) She had learned that *Jesus' approval was her priority*; therefore, she could handle her sister's disapproval.
c) She was *committed* to her priority; nothing could deter her from what she knew was most important of all.

Which of these three prerequisites for peace is hardest for you to fulfill in your everyday life? Check one *only*, the one *most* difficult for you to live, then share with your group:
_____a. Realizing that the main goal of your life is your personal relationship with God
_____b. Putting God's approval above the approval of others
_____c. Keeping your commitment to the priority you believe in

12. We will discuss these concepts in our next session. Pray about this issue of personal priority. (*Facilitator*: Close your time together with sentence prayers, praying for one another.)

*For next week*: Write the answers for chapter 2, #2 in your book before your next scheduled meeting together. Although this material will benefit you most if you come prepared, it also is designed to be productive for spontaneous group discussion without preparation. Come whether or not you've done the lesson in advance. It's an opportunity to grow.

## Footnotes:

1. *New Bible Commentary*, edited by Davidson; (Grand Rapids, Mich.: Eerdmans, 1960), p.851.

# 2
# *My Commitment to Listening to God*

Anchoring is step one in any situation of your life. As I look back over the agitated times of my life, I can see clearly that my mind and heart, my motives and desires, were not centered on my relationship with God. At those times, I had moved away from my Vertical Center (upward to God).

For me, the most difficult of the three prerequisites of having the peace and centeredness Mary had is "b" (Chapter 1, question 11): "She had learned that Jesus' approval was her priority; therefore, she could handle her sister's disapproval." Thinking of the opinions and thoughts others have toward me has caused me many agitations: anxiety, anger, even sadness. Undoubtedly some of this was totally unfounded, for I've learned that others are often wondering about my approval while I'm wondering about theirs.

But this understanding has not brought the freedom "centering" has. When I am aware and choose to seek the Lord's approval only, then I experience a kind of relaxation that is, for me, supernatural.

I do not mean to say that all strong emotions are what I refer to as "agitation." Jesus experienced strong feelings: Luke 13:34; John 11:33-35; Mark 14:32-34; Matthew 9:35-36; Matthew 15:7-9.

1. Read aloud the verses. Then list the strong emotions of Jesus recorded in the passages:

_____

_____

_____

Jesus could feel the whole range of God-given normal human emotions, but never become sinfully agitated. Never for one second did He doubt God's love or caring; never did He feel that life was out of control. He was always deeply aware that God was active in all His life situations, that His Father was Sovereign, that He was safe.

He also always kept the long-run of eternity permeating His viewpoint. He never allowed the day-by-day frustrations of human-ness, of limitedness and neediness, make Him doubt His God. Even in the agony of the garden, He gave His sorrow to the Father and submitted, trusting in His Father's control: "Yet not what I will, but what You will." On the cross, His last breath was, "Father, into Your hands I commit My spirit."

2. The Gospels often refer to the way Jesus related to His Father. This relationship is the key to His constant centeredness, His an-chor even in times of distress and strong emotion. Read the Scrip-ture below; list next to each the way Jesus was relating to His Father.

John 5:19,20,30

_____

_____

John 4:34; 6:38

_____

_____

John 7:16-18

_____

_____

John 8:16

_____

_____

John 10:14,15

_____

_____

(In the following verses Jesus compares His relationship with the Father to our relationship with Him.)

John 10:37,38

_____

_____

John 12:49,50

_____

_____

The Gospel of John often refers to Jesus' relationship with His Father. The writer was the "beloved disciple," the closest friend Jesus had on earth. John knew what made Jesus tick.

Though we are sinful and Jesus was not, I believe God wants us to have a measure of the kind of peace Jesus had on earth. Just last week I was very agitated. I got a severe sinus headache and woke up in the middle of the night thinking about the situation that upset me. I communicated with the persons involved and, although I know that was the right thing to do, it was helpful only to some extent. In fact, after one of the interactions, I felt more agitated!

In this case, a flood of assurance and peace came to me when the Holy Spirit gifted me with a deep conviction that God is the only one I need to please. His approval, my very personal relationship with Him, is #1. Others may be displeased with me—in my estimation not meeting my needs—but the bottom line of my life is the Lord and I. That's the bottom line of the abundant life, the life Jesus lived and the life He longs for us to live.

It's significant that although the situation I just referred to has not changed, I'm thinking straight now. I'm more oriented toward God's approval than man's. I'm looking to God. It's liberating and peaceful. I'm very grateful. I didn't come to this easily; it came through doing my part in journaling, prayer and choosing to trust. Through these processes, the Lord was free to speak to me. I'll tell you more about journaling later.

3. Let's work together now on defining "agitation" and "centeredness"—opposite positions in the Christian life. It's actually a continuum; that is, at any given moment, you are someplace on the line between agitation and peaceful centeredness. It looks like this:

agitation                                                    centeredness

The goal is to move toward being increasingly centered in your life. To better understand this concept, list below as many words or phrases you can think of that describe *agitation* and *centeredness*. Don't be concerned if you do not come up with too many on your own. This kind of exercise is best done in the context of the community of believers, because the experience is, for each of us, very personal, and therefore unique. It's colored by your concept of God and your concept of yourself.

I have listed some of mine so that I can share my personal experience with you.

| AGITATED | CENTERED |
| --- | --- |
| pulled apart | peaceful |
| fragmented | at rest |
| frightened | anchored |
| | vertical |
| | unshaken |

If you are studying this in a group, by sharing your ideas your perceptions and understanding will be enriched. Listen carefully to the words and phrases used by others. They will help you know God better and also deepen the fellowship among your group.

4.  The Bible expresses centeredness in various ways.
Read John 15:4, 9-10. Write the descriptions recorded in these verses:

_____

_____

The King James translation refers to centeredness as "abiding in Christ." Notice in verses 9 and 10 how Jesus compares His relationship with the Father to His desired relationship with us. Another reference to the resting attitude is found in Matthew

11:27-30. After reading this Scripture, write the contrast between the two states described there.

Listen to this passage in the *Amplified New Testament*: "Come to Me, all you who labor and are heavy-laden and over-burdened, and I will cause you to rest—I will ease and relieve and refresh your souls. Take My yoke upon you, and learn of Me; for I am gentle (meek) and humble (lowly) in heart, and you will find rest—relief, ease and refreshment and recreation and blessed quiet—for your souls. For My yoke is wholesome (useful, good) not harsh, hard, sharp or pressing, but comfortable, gracious and pleasant; and My burden is light and easy to be borne."

Now compare the states of agitation and centeredness with the states of Mary and Martha described in Luke 10:41,42:

_____

_____

_____

Read Colossians 2:19. The context here is the disintegration that comes to the Body when its members are not abiding in Christ. What phrase is used to describe centeredness?

_____

_____

_____

I think of books I read early in my Christian journey: *In His Steps*, by Charles M. Sheldon, asking constantly, "What would Jesus do?"; and *The Practice of the Presence of God*—Brother Lawrence's effort to remain centered.

No matter how we seek to express this concept, the important fact is that when we're agitated, we're not abiding in Christ.

Agitation is a sure sign we need to remind ourselves to relate *first* to Him, take on His yoke *only*, to be connected to the Head, to listen to Jesus.

In case you're identifying increasingly with the agitated attitude of Martha, let me assure you of the warmth and love of Jesus toward us, even when we're agitated. In John 11:5, John records the relationship Jesus had with Martha: "Jesus loved Martha and her sister and Lazarus." Christ understands our lack of faith, though He longs for us to have more.

The kind of freedom from agitation we've been talking about doesn't come primarily from our actions during an agitating situation. The freedom is more an outgrowth of a style of living, *a commitment to listening to the Lord* as Mary did. Mary was a listener to God. She had *chosen* to put God's approval before anyone else's. She had *chosen* to commit herself to listening to Jesus as her way of life, to do what was necessary to remain centered.

This chapter is designed to help you think about your first priority in life and to *choose* the behaviors necessary to remain true to your choice.

"Martha, Martha," the Lord answered, "you are worried and upset about many things, but only one thing is needed. Mary has *chosen* what is better, and it will not be taken away from her" (Luke 10:41,42).

5. Our potential for resting in Christ, for centering in any given situation of life, depends on our personal knowledge of God. The more we know who He really is and are committed to Him, the more potential we have for being anchored, no matter how difficult the situation. A.W. Tozer emphasized this when he wrote that what matters most is one's concept of God.

Read Philippians 3:7-10. In your own words, write Paul's deep desire:

_____

_____

If you had the depth of desire and commitment Paul experienced to know Christ, how would this show itself in your behavior? What would you be doing?

_____

_____

6. Look back at the life situations of Sharon, Sandy, Clare, Karen and Sarah in chapter 1, page 17. How would a deep knowledge of God affect their approaches to their lives? What do you think? Apply this question especially to the one woman toward whom you feel the greatest understanding. (No pious platitudes, please— let's be honest and realistic. Would knowing God deeply make a difference? How?):

_____

_____

7. This question will be optional in sharing in group discussion, but important for you to do for your self-understanding. How would you rate your commitment to listening to Jesus, to your pursuit of knowing Him? Circle the number:

| 0 | 1 | 2 | 3 | 4 | 5 | 6 | 7 | 8 | 9 | 10 |
|---|---|---|---|---|---|---|---|---|---|----|
| not interested | | | | | moderately motivated | | | | totally committed | |

How does the degree of your commitment affect your actions: Do you spend time regularly listening to God through the Scriptures? Check the one closest to reality:

_____rarely                         _____occasionally
_____about 3 times/week       _____4 or 5 times/week
_____almost daily                _____daily.

How often would you say you eat? Check the one closest to reality:

_____rarely                         _____occasionally
_____about 3 times/week       _____4 or 5 times/week
_____almost daily                _____daily.

Does the amount of time you spend in the Scriptures indicate that the way you rated yourself in commitment is accurate? _____yes; _____no.

Are you satisfied with the frequency of your times with the Lord? _____yes; _____no.

On another sheet of paper, write a letter to the Lord, sharing your thoughts, feelings and commitment to Him regarding putting your relationship with Him first in your life. Tell Him what you're going to do about your commitment.

8. Pray about your commitment to your number 1 priority. (*Facilitator:* Spend some time in your group discussing this exercise. Those who want to may share their findings, their commitments. Or perhaps some will want to read their letters to the Lord. Sharing a commitment can be a way of cementing it. Close in a brief time of sentence prayers, having each one pray for themselves and for others in the group by name in regard to their commitment to their #1 priority.)

For an excellent book on nurturing the inner life in Christ, see *The Table of Inwardness*, by Calvin Miller, Inter-Varsity Press, 1984.

# 3
# *My #2*
# *Personal*
# *Priority*

Next to your relationship with God, the most important person in your life you need to relate to is yourself. This doesn't lead to self-centeredness. It's a matter of responsibility.

You are responsible for having a relationship with yourself. Jesus took this for granted when He stated the Great Commandment: "Love the Lord your God with all your heart, with all your soul, with all your strength and with all your mind; and Love your neighbor as yourself" (Luke 10:27).

In a number of other Scripture passages the relationship between self-love and love for others is connected. We are responsible for self-acceptance and self-love. Taking care of one's own interests, such as Philippians 2 mentions, frees us to be genuinely interested in the other person's needs. "Look *not only* on your own interests...." That you will care for your own needs is taken for granted.

Self-hatred and self-rejection make it impossible for a person to care truly for others. If I am not loving myself and taking care of myself, I am so needy that I become self-centered. Instead of giving to you and putting your interests above my own, I will be concentrating on what I think I need from you, on my expectations of you. I will be blinded by my own neediness and become self-centered. Self-hatred and self-rejection, so common today, are sins Satan loves. They paralyze us into self-centeredness.

1. Look again at the Great Commandment (Luke 10:27), then read each of the following passages: Ephesians 5:33, Philippians 2:4 and Galatians 5:13-15. Write the message you get from the verses about your relationship with yourself:

_____

_____

_____

Traditionally, we've not talked too much in the church about relating with ourselves. Basically, we've believed if you spend too much time thinking about yourself, you become self-centered. I don't believe this is true. I believe that as you become increasingly self-aware and take responsibility for your "findings," you become more sensitive to others. Then you can afford to forget yourself and your needs. You can give to others the same sensitivity and caring you extend to yourself.

Our fear of becoming self-centered has kept us from pursuing self-understanding and self-care. But deeper than this is our fear of what we'll find if we pursue self-awareness. We have had a tight system of denial. We've believed that Christians should not experience fear, sadness, anger, guilt.

If we've been honest enough to admit that we're afraid or angry, we've felt condemned, believing a Christian should not feel this way. I'm convinced some people have left the church because of this sense of condemnation, feeling they don't measure up. Others, knowing their "failures," remain at the periphery, never using their gifts, paralyzed by lack of acceptance of their humanness.

2.   Consider if in the past Christians believed it was unspiritual to admit or share their genuine feelings and thoughts. Do you agree this has been the case? What has been your experience?

_____

_____

_____

What do you think of the idea that if we're spiritual we will not experience certain emotions?

_____

_____

_____

Do you think if we spend time thinking about our deep feelings we'll become self-centered?

_____

_____

_____

3.   Read Ephesians 4:25-27. Write this passage in your own words:

_____

_____

_____

What happens to feelings we do not deal with, letting the sun go down on them? How do you think these undealt-with-feelings give the devil a foothold?

_____

_____

_____

4.  Psalm 51 is David's psalm of repentance, of returning to genuineness after his sins. He had lied to himself about what was inside; his behavior had revealed the truth. Nathan had confronted David with reality, so that David's tight system of denial was broken (see 2 Samuel 12 if you're unfamiliar with the narrative). Read Psalm 51:6. What is it that David realized God wants for him?

_____

_____

_____

What do you think "truth in the inner parts" means?

_____

_____

_____

I became a Christian at the age of nineteen, through a university ministry. In my early years as a Christian I picked up the idea that if I really put God first in my life and loved Him, my life would go smoothly and I would not have negative emotions. Of course, this is a totally unbiblical idea, evidenced by the lives of Jesus, Joseph and Paul, and by passages like James 1 and Romans 5. These make clear that life is not smooth for people obedient to God. Godliness is evidenced not by the absence of trouble or negative emotions, but by how I respond to these in my life.

Though this belief in the smooth life seems absurd, I'm convinced that most believers still are under its influence. It's one of those ideas the father of lies loves. This belief keeps us from being honest and makes us hide our true selves from one another. It also makes us feel falsely guilty, so we do not experience "*koinonia*" (a sense of closeness with other believers) when we need it most. Because we believe we shouldn't be experiencing troubles, we don't share them and get the support of the body.

We cannot even be honest with ourselves or with God in the privacy of our quiet place. No wonder we experience agitation. How can we find comfort when we do not admit distress? How can we find encouragement when we do not admit despair? How can we love when we do not admit anger?

5. Read Ephesians 6:10-18. Beginning in verse 14, the armor is described in detail. What is the first piece to be put on?

_____

_____

We believe this letter was written by Paul from a Roman prison. He was perhaps looking at a Roman guard while describing the armor. The belt was worn to hold up the tunic in battle. The soldier always wore a tunic and just before battle tucked it up. Thus, it would not encumber him, but leave him ready for action.

We can apply this in our lives by realizing how often we trip over our tunics in battle because we are not girt about by the belt of truth. We have to hide our real selves from one another, even if it means being dishonest. We must wear masks and be careful not to reveal the truth about ourselves.

We must pretend that everything is okay at home, when we know it isn't. We have to pretend we're trusting the Lord when we're scared to death. We smile when we need to cry. This basic lack of honesty in the inward parts gives Satan a foothold; we trip over our tunics and fall down. If we were just honest, we could stand firm.

How does our dishonesty cause us to trip and yield to Satan's temptations?

_____

_____

I'm convinced the main reason most of us spend so little time alone with ourselves and alone with God, without the blaring television or stereo, is because we're afraid of what's inside us; we're afraid of our true selves. Paul was not.

6. Paul knew what was inside himself and he let his real person show. Had he not chosen to reveal the truth about himself, I wouldn't feel the same affection for him. I also wouldn't feel as hopeful as I do that I can be like him in following the Lord. If he hadn't let me see his vulnerable spots, his moments of despair, I couldn't like him as much as I do. It's much easier to learn and follow someone you like and respect for being real.

Read the following passages. Below each write the feelings Paul was experiencing:

2 Corinthians 1:8

_____

2 Corinthians 6:11, 12

_____

2 Corinthians 7:5

_____

2 Corinthians 7:6

_____

2 Corinthians 12:7-10

_____

Paul doesn't make himself out to be without humanness, does he? He shares his fears, conflicts, despair and affection and he asks the Corinthians to do the same. Paul was not afraid of his inner man. He wasn't afraid of letting his converts see his struggles with sin and with his own flesh. Perhaps you're familiar with Romans 7 in which he shares his struggle and its intensity.

How could Paul be so honest? I believe it was because he was convinced of *agape* (unconditional) love. He knew God loved him and so he could afford to be honest with himself about his inner man. Even Paul's inner man was deeply loved and redeemed by Christ. "Therefore, there is now no condemnation for those who are in Christ Jesus, because through Christ Jesus the law of the Spirit of life set me free from the law of sin and death" (Rom.8:1).

Paul understood redemption, and he understood *agape* love. He longed for all believers under his guidance to understand it too. He knew if they could taste of God's love for them, they would more easily respond by loving Him in return and obeying Him.

7. Read Paul's prayer for the Ephesians in 3:14-21. List what Paul asks God to do for them:

_____

_____

_____

Notice Paul's reference to the "inner being." He is recognizing that here is the place of God's deepest work. David recognized God's desire for truth in our inward parts. Paul is asking God to empower the Ephesians' inner beings through the Holy Spirit, so that Christ could be at home in their hearts through their faith. And their faith in Him would grow as they understood how very much He loved them.

8. Paul was very convinced of God's *agape* love and he understood that such love involves unconditional acceptance toward us, even though God knows the truth about us. Paul wanted every believer to understand this, for it would result in love for God and love for others.

Read Romans 15:7. What kind of acceptance was Paul telling the Romans to have toward each other even in their disagreement, and also toward Gentiles?

_____

_____

_____

How do you think accepting others as Christ has accepted us brings praise to God?

_____

_____

_____

9. How certain are you that God accepts you exactly as you are? (This section will be optional for sharing, so be as self-revealing as you can be.) Ask the Holy Spirit to speak to your spirit to let you know how much you understand and accept this truth of God's *agape* love for you. Circle the number that seems to be

your measure of understanding *agape*. God accepts _____ (fill in your name here) exactly as she is, even in her inner being.

| 0 | 1 | 2 | 3 | 4 | 5 | 6 | 7 | 8 | 9 | 10 |
|---|---|---|---|---|---|---|---|---|---|----|

I do not believe this.

I am finding this hard to believe.

I'm not totally convinced, but it's coming.

I know this deep inside me

10. Using another sheet of paper, write a letter from God to you. He is writing to tell you about His love for you. He is writing to assure you that He knows you deeply and loves and accepts you as you are. Begin your letter with "My dear (your name)".

11. Numbers 9 and 10 were for personal self-understanding. Complete this sentence: "In doing these two exercises, I learned this about myself:

_____

_____

_____

(*Facilitator*: Spend a few minutes talking about what you learned. Those who would like to share with the group may.)

12. (*Facilitator*: Close your time together today in silent prayer, having each person talk to the Lord. After five minutes have passed, offer a short sentence prayer to end the session.)

# 4
# My
# Commitment to
# Listening to
# Myself

In the last chapter we talked about the fear we have about what is inside us—our deepest motives, thoughts and feelings. Do you think you have listened to your inner being lately? The Holy Spirit of God dwells within you; He is aware of all that goes on inside you, even the depths you're not aware of yourself. That's a scary thought if it were not for the cross, if it were not for *agape* love.

Because of Christ, you can run boldly into the presence of God, exactly as you are. Because of *agape*, you can take the risk of shedding those protective layers that cover your inner self. You can stop hiding from yourself. Because God loves you, you can admit the truth to yourself. You can pursue to know yourself, a terrifying pursuit without God. Let's look at the scriptural concept of this inner person inside you.

1.   Read 1 Corinthians 2:11. What do you learn about ''a man's spirit within him?''

_____

_____

_____

This Scripture lets us know that very personal thoughts which only we ourselves can know are within each of us.

2.   What do you think would be some benefits to knowing what is deep inside you?

_____

_____

_____

3.   Read Psalm 139:23,24. What is the Psalmist's request of God?

_____

_____

_____

Why does David want God to reveal his heart? What would be the benefits to him?

_____

_____

_____

God cannot lead you in the way everlasting when you're not aware of your true motivations. He cannot free you from what you do not acknowledge. That's the meaning of the word "confess," which is defined as "agreeing with God." God already knows what is in you.

Psalm 139 talks about God's intimate knowledge of our thoughts before we think them, of our words before we speak them. "Where can I go from your Spirit? Where can I flee from your presence?...You created my inmost being...." David knew that God knew him through and through. David was asking the Lord to show him his inner being so that he could be healed, so that he could be changed to walk in the way everlasting.

This is the main benefit of self-awareness: healing and freedom—healing of the fear and hopelessness and freedom to be the person God created you to be. God wants you to be released from the bondage of denial and to experience the freedom of genuineness. "Thou desirest truth in the inward parts" (Ps. 51:6).

You ought to be more afraid of the results of hiding behind your protective layers than of increasing self-understanding. To understand your*self* is to be free from bondage to yourself.

4. What is your honest response to this idea of getting to know your inner being? What do you feel about it?

_____

_____

_____

5. Are you convinced that pursuing self-understanding pleases God? If so, why? If not, why not?

_____

_____

_____

Read Psalm 4:4.

6. Read Hebrews 4:9-16. The context of this passage is the record of God's offer of rest to the Israelites, which "they were not able to enter because of their unbelief" (Heb. 3:19). The passage says that God's rest is still available to us, that we are to "make every effort to enter that rest." The "rest" referred to here is the special and uninterrupted fellowship with the Father and the Son, offered to us as believers, which is in contrast to the merely weekly Sabbath fellowship under the Law.[1]

You remember that in earlier chapters we talked about "agitation." This is the opposite of uninterrupted fellowship with God. Agitation interrupts your rest, your easy yoke, which is rest for your soul. Agitation is rooted in unbelief.

Hebrews 4 is a significant passage in understanding how to have rest. Our lack of rest is usually caused by:
a)  our lack of self-awareness
b)  not approaching the throne of grace with our real needs
c)  not believing Him to be sufficient
Let's study this passage carefully.

7. After telling us to make every effort to enter this rest, the author begins to talk about the Word of God. Describe what he says in verse 12:

_____

_____

_____

We could put it simply by saying that the Scriptures tell us the truth about ourselves; a quiet reading of them with the ministry of the Holy Spirit will help reveal what's going on inside you. Can you think of a time when you experienced self-revelation, that is, you realized something was going on inside you that you were previously unaware of?

_____

8.  Read Proverbs 20:27. Write the verse in your own words:

9.  Now go back to Hebrews 4. In the context of telling us to work hard at entering God's fellowship of rest, the writer talks about the power of the Word of God to make us self-aware. Why do you think he does this? How are self-awareness and entering God's rest related?

10.  Think back to our five friends—Sharon, Sandy, Clare, Karen and Sarah. Each has hidden hurts, hidden needs. How can God meet needs you are not aware of, needs that are not realized and therefore do not cause you to run into God's presence to find grace in your time of need? Read again the five problem situations. Concentrate on the woman toward whom you feel the most understanding. What do you think are some of her hidden thoughts and attitudes? What does she need from God?

11. Write a self-disclosing prayer as though you were that woman. How could she "approach the throne of grace with confidence, so that she could receive mercy and find grace to help her in her time of need"? Write her prayer: "O God...

_____

_____

_____

(*Facilitator*: Have your group share some of these together.)

12. Read Psalm 62:1,5-8. What do you think it means to "pour out your hearts to Him"?

_____

_____

_____

How does this relate to finding rest in God alone?

_____

_____

_____

13. Resting is the opposite of agitation. Resting is being centered/anchored. It's a place of peace in any situation. Resting is rooted in relationship. This relationship is deep, nurtured through a commitment to consistent communication. This means time alone, alone with God and alone with you. You must know both God and yourself to have a deep relationship. Spending time alone is imperative. Look at Luke 4:42, 5:15-16. Jesus was under constant demands from people. How did He respond?

_____

_____

_____

Most people, when challenged to spend time alone communicating with God and with themselves, begin to recite their busy schedules. Jesus had the opposite response. It seems the more demands upon Him, the more He chose to keep His priorities.

Martin Luther once said he had so much to do in a day that, to get everything done, he needed to spend several hours in prayer before the activities began. I seem to respond the opposite way; the busier I get, the more likely my time alone with God and with Marilyn gets shorter or snuffed out entirely. I've learned this is entirely self-defeating. I begin eventually to feel my agitation, my lack of resting, my unbelief. It's possible for me to get agitated even when I have spent time alone, but much more likely when I haven't.

Nothing magic goes on in a "quiet time." But it's strategic because the Christian life is all about relationship: relationship with God, with myself and then with others. Jesus summed it up in the Great Commandment. And He said, "Do this and you will live" (Luke 10:27,28). You will have the abundant life He came to give if you keep these priorities in line.

14. I hope you're convinced of these priorities in your life. A method I've found personally very helpful in my time alone is journaling. There are many ways to journal. What do you know about journaling?

_____

_____

_____

Journaling is a way of listening to God and listening to yourself, to your inner being. I often combine it with reading the Scriptures, but not always. I keep a notebook to record my spiritual and emotional journey through life. Sometimes I copy a Scripture verse into my notebook and write what God has said to me through that passage.

Other times I write pages and pages about my feelings and thoughts and about what is going on in my life, in my relationships and in my head. Those pages often end with my writing a prayer to the Lord. "What shall I do about this, Lord? I am in bondage to my feelings. Free me, my Father, I am willing."

I never censor my writing. God knows anyway, so what's the point? Writing the truth helps me take responsibility for reality, and I find healing. You cannot have healing for what you do not expose to the light. My journaling never leaves me hopeless. I feel I have more of a handle on a situation, even though I may still have the feelings and may not yet know how to deal with the issue. Putting my experience on paper is, for me, a road to management of my life and to resting in God. Journaling is a form of "pouring out my heart before Him." If privacy is a problem for you, find a safe place to keep your journal so you can write freely.

To give you an idea of what a journal might look like, I'm going to write for Sarah, the 47-year-old with one married daughter and two children in college:

"Sue just called. She's having trouble potty training Timmy. I'm so full of feelings. What is it? What is crying out inside me? Lord, help me to understand. Is it grief? The loss of years never to be lived again. That's it. I'm thinking of the times with Sue, and Carl and Ken. I'm crying, Lord. Those times are gone forever. They'll never need me again like that. I'm angry about this. Lord, I am really angry. Forgive me. I think I have my fist in Your face. Why? Why? I felt so needed by them, so loved, so important. I can't believe this. It's irrational, but it's exactly how I feel. What am I to do with these feelings, Lord? "Will you meet my need to be important? Is there something I can do for You, Lord? For Your people? Please guide me, Father. I feel desperate. Give me the courage to share this with Stan. Please don't let him laugh."

15.   How do you feel toward Sarah, now that you've seen a glimpse of her inner feelings?

_____

_____

_____

16.   On another sheet of paper do some journaling about a very distressing situation in your life. Tell the Lord exactly how you feel. (*Facilitator*: These will not be shared unless someone has a strong desire to do so.)

17.   Close your time today by rereading Hebrews 4:10-16. (*Facilitator*: Share prayer requests together. Close in brief sentence prayers of support for one another.)

Two books that give excellent ideas on journaling: *Ordering Your Private World*, by Gordon MacDonald, Moody Press, 1984 (especially pages 140-47). *Friend to Friend*, by Stone and Keefauver, available from Group Books, Box 481, Loveland, Colo. 80539.

For further discussion of Hebrews 4, see *Acceptance*, by Walter A. Henrichsen, Navpress, Colorado Springs, Colo.

Footnote:

1.   *Vine's Expository Dictionary of New Testament Words*, (Nashville, Tenn.: Royal Publishers, Inc.), p.960.

# 5
# *My #3 Personal Priority*

Out of the richness of your relationship with God and your relationship with yourself will overflow love for others. When you spend time with the Lord and with yourself, you'll be ready for your third priority of life: your relationship with others.

Who are these others? First are the closest persons in your life. If you're married—your husband. If you're single—your closest friend (this could be a relative or nonrelative). Then comes your other relationships, your loved ones, your friends and finally those you would like to love into the Kingdom.

We all have levels of relationships in our lives, relationships of varying depths and degrees of closeness. Jesus did. We're going to begin this section by looking at His relationships.

1. Read John 13:21-25. Who is this "disciple whom Jesus loved?" What do you know about him?

_____

_____

Read John 19:25-27. What do you learn about John here?

_____

_____

_____

2.  The person closest to Jesus on earth was the disciple John. Jesus trusted His mother's welfare into His friend's hands. After John, two other disciples follow as close companions to Jesus. They were Peter and John's brother James. Only these three were privileged to be with Jesus at His transfiguration. Read Mark 9:2. They were the same intimate ones who shared in one of His most needy moments of human existence and spiritual anguish—in Gethsemane.

Read Mark 14:32-34 and Matthew 26:36-38. Why do you suppose Jesus left most of the disciples in one part of the Garden, taking only the three with Him to where He was going to spend time with His Father?

_____

_____

_____

What do you think Jesus needed from His close friends?

_____

_____

_____

3.   Apart from the cross, Gethsemane was Jesus' most deeply painful moment on earth. In Hebrews 5:7 we get more information about His tears and loud cries to His Father. His anguish was very personal, but He shared it with His close friends. How do you feel about sharing your deepest anguish and loud tears with another person?

_____

_____

_____

4.   This is for personal use only. It will not be shared in your group. Do you have someone you can cry with about your deepest pains in life?

_____yes      _____no      _____to some extent.

How satisfied are you with the level of sharing in your closest relationship? Circle the number which best describes your feelings:

| | | | | | | | | | |
|---|---|---|---|---|---|---|---|---|---|
| 1 | 2 | 3 | 4 | 5 | 6 | 7 | 8 | 9 | 10 |

not satisfied                                         very satisfied

If you are not satisfied, why do you think this is?

_____

_____

_____

Do you want someone to share deeply with in your life?
_____yes      _____no      _____unsure

What do you think you could do to make it possible for you to be very open with the close person(s) in your life? Notice that this question says: what can *you* do? Perhaps you feel that if the other person were more understanding or supportive or open, you could share. But the qualities of the other persons did not stop Jesus. His close friends failed Him. Nevertheless, they remained His close friends to the end. He shared with them, though He probably suspected, or even knew, they would not come through for Him. What do you think you could do to make it possible for you to be this open with the close person(s) in your life?

---

---

---

5.   What are some reasons that even in the closest relationships people often do not share deeply? List as many as you can:

---

---

---

6.   One factor most destructive to close relationships and also most common is our desire to change the other person. Why do you think we have such a strong motivation to seek to change other people, especially those closest to us?

---

---

One reason we try to change others is because we think that if they change they will better meet our needs. It is true we have needs that can only be met in the context of relationship. God made us this way. Even when Adam had a perfect relationship with God, before he sinned, God declared that Adam needed a close person in his life. It is important to have close relationships in our lives.

However, one reason so many close relationships are unsatisfying—and why we try to change the other person—is because we expect the impossible. Our expectations of marriage, for example, are impossible to fulfill, thus the divorce rate rises; or, as in the case of many believers, we stick it out, feeling deeply unhappy inside.

7.   What do you think might be some expectations people have of marriage and close relationships that cannot be fulfilled in this way?

_____

_____

_____

David Grant, author of *The Ultimate Power*, observes, "Apart from God's unconditional love we are all in a neurotic pursuit of a sense of worth. We feel we must be worthy to be loved. And to be worthy we must perform. I believe that everything we do is an effort to get love or because we are loved."[1]

We all are in a neurotic pursuit, searching for a sense of worth and for love. And, of course, we already have worth and are so very loved. God has given us both. But we want to be declared significant, valuable and loved by those close people in our lives. And when they do not come through, we find ourselves agitated.

Our expectations drive these close people from us. The agitation between us—either outward conflict or silent coldness or the miriad of degrees between—distances our significant people from us. Then even these close relationships cannot meet our needs as God intended.

All because we have demanded from a human relationship what only God can do: give us a deep sense of our worth and love us unconditionally. No one on earth can do this for us. One way we drive wedges between ourselves and others is in our pursuit of their approval. We believe we'll feel better about ourselves if we get the approval of the important people in our lives. The Scripture says a great deal about this. Obviously a human need is to receive approval.

8. Jesus spoke of this choice between seeking from God or seeking from men. He spoke to the Jews of their orientation to the horizontal (outward to man) rather than to the vertical (upward to God). Read John 5:41, 44 and John 12:42-43. Write Jesus' description of their motivation:

_____

_____

_____

Matthew 6:1 records another of Jesus' statements on this issue. Write it in your own words:

_____

_____

_____

9. Paul is aware of this struggle, this choice. Read Galatians 1:10 and 1 Thessalonians 2:4. Do you identify with what Paul is saying? How? What does it feel like to be trying to please men, to be striving after their approval?

_____

_____

_____

10. For personal use only: If God were to come and sit next to you right now, what do you think He would say to you about those close people in your life? About what you want from them? Write His words to you here: "My dear (your name)_____

_____

_____

_____

11. We're going to close by thinking about Dave Grant's statement quoted earlier: "I believe everything we do is an effort to get love or because we are loved." What do you think Dave meant by this?

_____

_____

_____

If we were permeated by the assurance of God's love for us, this would be our motivation in all of life and in all our relationships. We would not need to be hungrily pursuing love and thus distancing people in our lives.

12. Read Deuteronomy 7:7-9, Psalm 103:1-14, Psalm 63:3, 2 Thessalonians 2:16, Jude 21. (_Facilitator_: Close today by having these passages read aloud, one after the other. Pray that everyone will leave with a heightened awareness of God's personal love for them.)

Two excellent pamphlets for your group: *Improving Your Self-Image*: The Open-Church Foundation, 58 Middle Mt., Gloucester, Mass. 01930.

*You Are Really Somebody*, by J. Allan Petersen, available from Family Concern, 1415 Hill Ave., Wheaton, IL 60187.

Each includes an extensive prayer that can be used daily to permeate your mind with the knowledge of God's personal love for you.

Footnotes:
1. David Grant, author of *The Ultimate Power*, quoted in *Solo*, Nov./Dec., 1980.

# 6
# My Commitment to Listening to Others

I've enjoyed sharing with you and have learned a great deal in preparing this material. This last chapter is important. How we treat other people is where the rubber meets the road in terms of how Christianity is reflected in our lives. It's not easy to love.

You've probably heard of the "love man," Leo Buscaglia. His popularity evidences the quest for love we talked about in our last chapter. Leo got started on his love message through a tragic event in his teaching career at the University of Southern California. A beautiful, intelligent and sensitive student of his committed suicide: everything going for her, but no desire to live. Reevaluating the teaching offered at the university, Buscaglia decided to offer a class called "Love, 1A."

"You see, what bothers me," he explained, " is that there is a course in everything but what is truly essential. Nobody teaches people to be people. Nobody teaches you what to do with loneliness and despair. You're supposed to be an expert in getting along with others. Well, that's just hogwash, because we don't have the skills, we don't know what to do. And when we find ourselves in those positions, we panic. Then, simple despair becomes neurosis and psychosis, and people kill themselves."[1]

Christians need training in love too. Many times the reality is that our relationships aren't any more loving than those without Christ. In the *Standard* magazine, research is cited that reveals religious couples are 42 percent less likely to divorce. Yet they report they are no more or no less happy in their marriages than couples with no strong attachment to religion.[2]

In other words, religious couples are more committed, but not necessarily more loving or close. We all know of churches riddled with internal conflict, believers fighting with believers. And most likely, everyone of us has broken or distressed personal relationships in our past or present.

We need help. We need a "Love, 1A" course from the Lord. Consequently, I would like to leave you with one very practical way you can begin to be a more loving person. I know you share my desire to be so.

1. Let's begin by looking at some Scriptures that speak to this issue of relating to others. Read 1 John 3:21-24. This passage is talking about effectiveness in prayer. We can have confidence in prayer when we are obedient to His commands. Write His commands:

_____

_____

_____

How important in terms of our effectiveness in prayer is the way we relate to other people?

_____

_____

Why do you think God has made a stipulation to prayer-power, relating to how we love others?

_____

_____

_____

2.   Read John 15:9-17. Several benefits are promised to those disciples of Christ, like you and me, who love one another. List them:

_____

_____

_____

This is an impressive list, isn't it? Jesus is emphasizing here, in His last discourse, what really counts to Him: that we love one another.

3.   Read John 13:34,35. In the previous passages we saw the results of loving one another: confidence in prayer, remaining in Christ's love, inner joy that is complete joy, being God's friend and bearing fruit that will last. In this passage is another benefit stated by Jesus. What is it?

_____

_____

_____

Now take the list of six items and rewrite each in your own words:

_____

_____

_____

4.   Even with all these motivating advantages to loving others, it's not easy to be a loving person. Love shows itself in behavior. Write a list of actions you believe are ways to love another person:

_____

_____

_____

5.   The people in our lives most difficult to show these actions toward are our immediate family. Why do you think this is?

_____

_____

_____

6.   There is one loving action that can transform any relationship. Even the most distressed relationship can show a marked difference when one member takes this action of love: _listening!_ Although listening is the first God-given communication skill we can see operative very early in life, it is the last we receive any training for.

Communication is the bedrock of any relationship, and listening is the first and most foundational of all communication skills. We need four basic skills to communicate: speaking, listening, writing and reading.

List the order in which these are covered in our educational process (which is taught first, second, etc.?):

_____

_____

_____

Do you remember receiving any training in listening during your schooling?

_____

_____

7.  Listening is absolutely basic to the whole process of loving. Do you agree? What is the relationship between feeling loved and knowing someone understands you because they have listened to you?

_____

_____

_____

8.  Besides the fact that we rarely are trained for this vital skill, other blocks stop effective listening. What do you think are some reasons it is difficult to fully attend to another person and listen? What do you think the average person is doing while the other person is talking?

_____

_____

_____

9. Look at Proverbs 18:2,13. In both Scripture verses two actions are contrasted. What are they?

_____

_____

Yes, talking and listening are definitely opposites. Perhaps you've read about the experience of Rhea Zakich. She was a Christian mother, wife of twelve years, active in her church and community. Forced silence because of a throat problem brought her new life. For the first time in her life, she *had* to listen; she could not talk. Out of her silence came the powerfully effective communication game, the *Ungame*. Still unable to talk, she and her family were playing the game on the handmade board at home.

She drew a card that evoked a very honest answer from her son. Taking her tablet, she wrote, "Why is it that you share so much in this game. But when I used to ask you these things, you would just grunt?"

"Well, Mom," her son replied, "in the game we know you won't *say* anything!"

Rhea says she learned more in 20 minutes sitting around the *Ungame* than she had learned about her family in 12 years.[3]

10. What is your response to Rhea's experience?

_____

_____

_____

11. Most of us are just waiting for our turn to talk instead of attending to what the other person is sharing. Listeners are in such short supply that many people will pay a stranger $50 an hour to listen to their deepest feelings. True, at times we need a professional to help us sort out our lives. But I'm convinced

that a great deal of therapy is meant by God to be experienced across the breakfast table and the communion table. We have a debt to love one another. Loving means listening. Read James 1:19-20. Rewrite these verses in your own words:

_____

_____

_____

_____

12.  God is revealing a relationship between listening, speaking and anger. How do you think they are related?

_____

_____

_____

A great deal of our anger is based on misunderstanding. That is, we think in some way the other person is against us, discounting us, not caring for us, etc. How could listening correct these misperceptions?

_____

_____

_____

13.  You probably have read this saying: "I know you believe you understand what you think I said, but I'm not sure you are aware that what you heard is not what I meant." Can you think of an example when this happened between you and someone else? Write how the misunderstanding occurred:

_____

_____

_____

14.   Dietrich Bonhoeffer, in his book *Life Together*, wrote: "The first service that one owes to others consists of listening. Just as love to God begins with listening to His Word, so the beginning of love for one another is to listen to them."[4]

We started this study by looking at the Great Commandment (Luke 10:27,28). Loving means listening. In Section I we talked about listening to God; Section II, listening to ourselves; and Section III, listening to others. Which of these is hardest for you to do?

_____

_____

_____

In which area would you most like to grow and change?

_____

_____

_____

What steps could you take in the next six months to help you grow in this area?

_____

_____

_____

Will you do it?_____yes _____no

15. Pray that God will help you to be a better listener to God, to yourself and to others.

(*Facilitator*: Go around your group, each sharing in which area she most wants to grow and change. Close your time together praying for one another in these longings to be better listeners to God, to yourselves and to others.)

NOTE: Sometimes being accountable to a fellow believer is an excellent motivator to grow. If you would like to continue to share with someone in your group and work on goals together, I urge you to take the risk. Ask that person to meet weekly with you for a committed time of three months. Later you can decide if you want to stop or continue. Take the risk. If you are not studying this in a group, try to find someone to share with. You will grow from it.

An excellent book for your enrichment in regard to listening: *Listening, A Christian's Guide to Loving Relationships*, by Norman Wakefield, Word Books, 1981.

Footnotes:

1. Leo Buscaglia, *Chicago Tribune Magazine*, Nov. 28, 1982, pp.43-56 (quote, p. 48).
2. *The Standard*, June 1984, p.5.
3. *Psychology for Living*, July/Aug., 1983, pp.6,7,24 (quote, p.24).
4. Dietrich Bonhoeffer, *Life Together*, (New York: Harper & Row, 1954), p.97.

# PART II:
# SAYING ''YES, GOD'' TO LIVING

## By Pamela Heim

# *Introduction*

Have you heard the one about the man whose will stipulated that after his death he was to go into his grave seated in his luxury car? Following his decease, his friends carried out his wish; they buried him in his Cadillac. At the interment a mourner, noting the unusual and magnificent "casket" said, "Man, that's really living!" Certainly the corpse was *not* living; he was dead in spite of the expensive trappings he took to his grave.

Some walking, talking people for all practical purposes are not really living either. They simply exist. They are putting in time until God calls them home to heaven. The qualities of warmth, vigor and vitality appear absent in them. Somewhere along the line they stopped growing. They ceased to change. They settled into routines.

Each woman in this situation has her own reasons for opting out of productive aliveness. I propose, however, that she gave up living and opted for mere existence because:

—she didn't have God's perspective on her days helping her to thoroughly explore the potential of each age and stage of her life;

—she selfishly and/or fearfully decided she could no longer give or serve;

—she let the pain of failure, loss and disappointment drive her into a protective, never-risk pattern of behavior.

In the following three chapters, you will take a good, hard look at the life of Moses. In doing so, you will discover that he was a man who really lived. At times it looked as if he went backward rather than forward, as if he were put on the shelf, as if he would give in to doubts about the possibility of his usefulness and success. But he overcame his temptation to an easy existence and went on to become the great leader and lawgiver of God's people.

As you see God's work in Moses' life, I trust you will find your faith strengthened so that you will say, "Yes, God!" to vigorous, vital living.

# 1
# *Living*
# *Is Now*
# *In Session*

As a topic of conversation, time is kind of like the weather. It's a safe, common subject for discussion with strangers as well as acquaintances. Folks who don't even know each other feel comfortable talking about how time flies, how there's not enough of it to do what needs doing and so on.

It's not unusual that people should keenly feel the march of time. Turning the pages of the calendar and watching the seasons change promotes an awareness that days are slipping away. Every holiday seems to catch us by surprise. "Can you believe Christmas is here already?" If our wrinkling and sagging bodies don't smack us in the face with the knowledge that years are passing, then talking to a teenager will.

As one whose fabulous 40th birthday is past, I am chagrined that younger generations look back on the '50s—my high school years, mind you—as an interesting, good ol' "Happy Days" era, *ancient history* as some see it. I find it a bit disconcerting to realize that the under-25 bunch can't share my memories of Kennedy's assassination, the first moon landing, the Vietnam war, or Nixon's resignation.

Israel's King David could identify with us in our time consciousness; he often spoke of the brevity of life. The psalmist said this brevity demands a proper evaluation of how we use our days. In fact, various Scriptures exhort us to use time well (e.g., Ephesians 5:16 and Colossians 4:5). Solomon noted that one should give thought to appropriate action with regard to time: "There is an appointed time for everything. And there is a time for every event under heaven" (Eccl. 3:1-8).

The Gospels reveal that Jesus was also time conscious. He was not only committed to doing the Father's will but also to doing it according to His Father's timetable. Though He referred often to the mission His Father had given Him, He didn't frantically race toward that goal. We never sense that He chafed at leaving an exciting, public ministry to the multitudes for a period of quiet, private time of ministry to a few.

Jesus impresses us with the way He lived each minute to the full. As a result, He accomplished an incredible volume of work, yet He never appeared hurried or hassled. He even took time to pray, relax and attend a wedding party.

If we are going to say, "Yes, God!" to living, we are going to have to hold His view of time. We must come to terms with the fact that there really is time enough to do all our Lord wants us to do. We will have to trust the days of our lives to His ordering.

## Refreshing Your Memory

Perhaps our greatest encouragement in this area is the life of Moses. So let's take a rather extensive look at his autobiography to see what he can teach us about gaining the divine perspective on our days and months and years. First we need to refresh our minds about the background facts of his life.

In the last chapters of Genesis, we read that the family of Jacob, also known as Israel, went to Egypt to avoid a famine in their country, Canaan. Because of the forgiving spirit of his son Joseph, Jacob and his eleven other sons and their wives and children found food and a home in Egypt.

When we come to Exodus, 400 years have passed since the children of Israel settled in Egypt's land of Goshen to avoid starvation in Canaan. The first chapter of Exodus explains three things that had happened during that four-century period. First, the population of the Israelites had grown from 70 people to probably about 2 or 3 million. We can't say exactly how many people because the Bible simply mentions 600,000 men—no one bothered to record the number of women and children (12:37).

The second fact mentioned is the paranoia of the Pharaoh. The ruler's fear was due to his country's many enemies. Egypt had become an empire through conquest. That hardly made for lots of good will toward it among the family of nations. Goshen, the area inhabited by the Israelites, lay between Egypt and its tributary-paying subjects. The Pharaoh was concerned that the Israelites would form an alliance with its foes and aid them in entering Egypt.

Third, Exodus 1 tells of the resulting persecution of the feared Israelite minority. To prevent more growth in population, Pharaoh ordered the death of all newborn Israelite males. This brings us to the story of Moses.

## Little Boat Person

When Moses was born, his Levite parents simply could not carry out the ruler's edict (2:1-4). They did not destroy their infant. However, after three months had passed, they discovered that they couldn't keep the healthy baby quiet enough to hide his existence. So they placed him in a specially prepared basket that they put on the Nile River. Stephen's sermon in Acts 7:21 explains what their intent was. Apparently they could not bring themselves to murder him outright, but they exposed him or put him out to die. They were not heartless; they were just desperate folks in a desperate situation.

Some have suggested that Amram and Jochebed knew God would somehow rescue their wee one. Scripture doesn't confirm this theory. Indeed, even believers in the Lord find themselves at times having to make unhappy but inevitable choices. They have no assurance that the Almighty will rescue them by changing their tragic situations.

The best they can do is hang on to the knowledge that He will see them through the circumstances. This is the essence of walking by faith and not by sight. It is trusting in the love, wisdom and power of God even when one can't possibly fathom anything loving or wise about His permitting certain situations.

For many Israelite parents in Egypt during that period, the Lord didn't come to the rescue of their male infants. Beautiful little boys died, killed by midwives and others. In the case of the baby floating in a wicker boat on the Nile, the Lord did intervene (2:5-8).

Here's how the little boat person survived. Pharaoh's daughter just happened to go to bathe when and where she did. She just happened to notice the basket and was curious. The baby just happened to cry and arouse her sympathy. His sister just happened to have the presence of mind and courage to offer their mother as nursemaid. The suggestion just happened to appeal to the woman.

Just happened? No way! It was all by God's design. It was a part of His plan for the Hebrew people.

A woman with a divine perspective on her life realizes there is no such thing as good fortune or bad luck. She knows that "with God things don't just happen; everything by Him is planned," as the song goes. She believes every circumstance she faces is in line with His purpose for her.

She recognizes that, as Catherine Marshall put it, "God is in everything. The events of our lives do come to us, moment by moment, as from His hands."[1] This includes the sad as well as the glad. In fact, the most godly people you have ever met would probably confess that the Lord has wonderfully used pain, perhaps more than pleasure, to shape them.

However, in the case of the Levite parents and their son, it pleased God to spare them grief and save the baby. Better yet, He even saw to it that the baby's own mother had the joy of rearing him until his weaning (2:9). Historians say that back then weaning a child was often deferred until he was three years old. Some commentators suggest that the boy may have lived with his parents until he was about seven before he was returned to Pharaoh's daughter, who adopted him and named him Moses.

## Training A Future Leader

The result of Moses' years with his birth mother was that she had the opportunity to instill her values in her son's formative little mind. She grounded him in a faith in Israel's God. She helped him understand his identity as a son of the covenant made to Abraham, Isaac and Jacob. I believe this is what happened —based on his later actions.

When the narrative continues in Exodus 2:10, forty years had passed. Again Stephen sheds some light on what transpired in those silent decades. Acts 7:21 and 22 say, "Pharaoh's daughter took him away and nurtured him as her own son. And Moses was educated in all the learning of the Egyptians, and he was a man of power in words and deeds."

Jewish tradition says that the Pharaoh did not have a son and that Moses stood to inherit the imperial throne of Egypt. Whether or not this was the case, Moses certainly would have received one of the finest educations in the world at the government's expense.

Zondervan's *Pictorial Bible Dictionary* tells us that "the court of Egypt provided educational facilities for royal heirs of tributary princes from city-states that were subject to Egyptian pharaohs. Consequently, Moses may have had classmates from as far as the Euphrates River...."

Moses probably studied geography, astronomy, law and government. Furthermore, the first forty years of his life taught him royal ways and court etiquette. In short, Moses gained the knowledge he needed to become the leader of a great nation. If one were to have looked for a Hebrew to lead the Israelites, one could not have found one more eminently qualified than Moses.

In the mature man we find evidence of his early years with his mother. As an adult, Moses identified with the people of his infancy. When he saw an Egyptian beating a Hebrew, he sided with the cause of the Hebrew (2:11-15). Why did he choose to stand with his oppressed people rather than live out an easier life as an adopted Egyptian prince, perhaps heir apparent?

Again Stephen explained this for us (Acts 7:23-25): "But when he was approaching the age of forty, it entered his mind to visit his brethren, the sons of Israel. And when he saw one of them being treated unjustly, he defended him and took vengeance for the oppressed by striking down the Egyptian. And *he supposed that his brethren understood that God was granting them deliverance through him*; but they did not understand" (italics mine).

## Battling Injustice

I think Moses sensed, even at that time, that God planned to use him to lead his people. I believe he knew it was God's will to use him to deliver the Israelites. Certainly many great people in the Bible had a sense of being set apart by the Lord for ministry from conception or birth.

For example, Paul believed the Lord had set him apart for ministry at the beginning of his life (Gal. 1:15). Isaiah said that God had formed him in the womb to be His servant (Isa. 49:1,5). Jeremiah heard God say that He had consecrated him before his birth (Jer. 1:4,5). Each felt a sense of divine destiny. I suggest that Moses also sensed this.

To be sure, each of us is a person with a divine purpose. Jesus Christ knew all about us before we first breathed. He understood all we would face and recognized our strengths and weaknesses. Psalm 139 is most clear about this. The Lord had and has a plan for our lives. As we cooperate with Him, we experience the joyful sense of destiny that gives us a zest for each stage and experience of life. In some way, everything that comes our way is all a part of His scheme of things.

Not only did Moses' sense of destiny lead to his murdering a man, I believe he killed the Egyptian because he was by character a man deeply concerned about justice. (We shall see this same quality in him in a later incident.) As a just man, he simply could not stomach the injustice inflicted upon the Hebrews.

Wanting fairness is good, but the problem was that Moses attempted to do God's will in his way and in his time. The Lord demands not only that we do His will, but that we do it according to His plan and timetable. Though Moses was willing to lead his people and acted to take on a leadership role among them, he was not ready at that point to assume leadership for a couple million people.

## Between A Rock And A Hard Place

So Moses became a *persona non grata* in Egypt. He was not accepted by the Israelites and had a death sentence placed on him by the Pharaoh. Between a rock and a hard place, Moses fled to Midian.

Midian was a son of Abraham by Keturah. The land of Midian, where his descendants lived, was east of the Jordan River and the Dead Sea and extended all the way down to the eastern and southern areas of the Sinai Peninsula in Moses' day.

Arriving in Midian, Moses saw another injustice. He saw some women being mistreated and came to their aid. They were the daughters of a priest in whose home Moses came to live. He married Zipporah, one of the daughters, and she bore him a son. Moses took up the vocation of a shepherd and tended his father-in-law's flock (2:16-22).

Any way you look at it, that was quite a comedown from a palace. It was as if Britain's Prince Charles were suddenly to find himself irrevocably slopping hogs for his livelihood. Leading sheep was a far cry from leading a nation of people. We read stories about the purity and fleeciness of lambs; but those who know sheep tell us they can be smelly, stupid and often noisy creatures.

Don't you wonder how Moses felt? It isn't too hard to imagine that he thought the work was beneath him. Or that he felt his Egyptian education was going to waste. And tending sheep was his lot not for just a few weeks or months. He was a shepherd in a wilderness for 40 years.

After four decades had passed, God spoke to the ex-prince-turned shepherd. He told him it was time for the Israelites to be delivered from Egyptian slavery. And the deliverer was to be none other than Moses himself (3:1-10).

Notice that the Lord spoke to Moses at Horeb. Mt. Horeb is another name for Mt. Sinai. Mt. Sinai or Horeb is the place where God later gave the Ten Commandments. We realize, then, that Moses was thoroughly familiar with the territory through which he would one day lead the Israelites. In fact, the Hebrews later camped at the spot of the burning-but-not-burned-up bush for about a year.

# Risking Change

Moses was 80 years old at the time of that incident. For him and his people it was the fulness of time. The Lord said, "I have surely seen the affliction of My people...and have given heed to their cry...." You see, what had been happening in Egypt had not escaped God's notice. He had not become aware of the situation of the Hebrews just prior to His visit to Moses. He had known all along what was going on under the Pharaoh. So why had God delayed? Why had He not allowed Moses to lead His people out of Egypt sooner? I suggest two reasons:

First, the Lord had to *ready* His people. Through the decades, as their misery grew greater and greater and their sense of hopelessness increased, so did their longing for a liberator. It is probable that, even though they had suffered much under the Egyptians, many of them would have been reluctant to leave the land of their oppression. Remember, they had lived there 400 years—more years than the settling of America by our ancestors.

It's been said we will choose the devil we know over the angel we don't know. Somebody has also suggested that if we could take all our problems and pile them in the middle of the floor, and then could pick out any problem to keep—most of us would choose the very same problems we had tossed into the pile.

That's because change is always risky and frightening. That's why we cling to the familiar and the known even when it causes unhappiness. Blaine Smith wrote, "There is...an inertia within us that resists change. This fact of human nature which psychologists call self-consistency is, I believe, closely related to or identical with what the Scriptures term 'hardness of heart.' Hardness of heart, in both the Old and New Testaments, always refers to people's inability (or refusal) to believe, in spite of the most convincing evidence, new insights which God has revealed to them. It affects both our attitude toward God and toward ourselves, stunting our growth in both areas."[2]

All this simply says that it takes a fairly horrendous amount of hurt before some people are willing to act to change their situations or to solve their problems. They don't risk something new until the old has become absolutely unbearable.

In the long period of their oppression, the Hebrews grew ever more unified in their wish to get away from their oppressors. Their desire heightened to solve their problem. In spite of that, you will remember that later when they were free of Egypt, many would have returned to slavery and to the food they had enjoyed there. The problems in Egypt seemed more tolerable to them than the unknown future with Moses. So we can see that God's delay in answering the cry of His people gave them the necessary time to become totally ready. They were willing to risk leaving the familiar country of their birth and venturing out into the unknown.

A story is told of two frogs hopping down a muddy country lane on their way to a pond. One frog slipped and fell into a deep rut. And in spite of his friend's encouragement and advice, the trapped frog could not jump out of his steep-banked prison. So the one frog continued by himself to hop down the road to the pond. A short time later, the frog who had been in the rut joined his friend in the water. When asked how he got out of the rut, he said, "I had to. A truck was coming."

Some of us may not get out of our ruts unless threatened by a truck, so to speak. Some of you reading this may be facing many difficulties, and you've been praying about them. Understand that God has an answer to your problems. But He may delay in sending that answer to you because you're not ready to hear it.

You may need to feel a lot more miserable before you are willing to trust the Lord and to accept His creative, perhaps unusual solutions. You may need to lose a little more confidence in yourself as being able to handle the situation alone. You may not be ready yet to take the leap of faith that will land you in the center of God's blessing on your life.

## God's Timetable

A second reason for the delay in rescuing the Israelites was that God had to prepare Moses. It took 80 years before Moses was qualified to live his last forty years in which he performed his most magnificent work for the Lord.

And so the Lord permitted Moses to wander over the Sinai Peninsula until he became a desert-wise man. He learned how to keep a big bunch of ignorant sheep in line and how to find them food and water. If one were to have looked for a Hebrew to lead a group of Israelites through a wilderness, one could not have found a more eminently qualified man than Moses.

Now how does understanding all this help us have a creative perspective on life so we can say, "Yes, God!" to all of life and appreciate and profit from each aspect of it?

First, to live fully we must understand that God is not in a hurry. He does all things well (Mark 7:37). His timetable is perfect (Eccl. 3:11). He is never too late and never too early. He is always on time.

How hard this is for us impatient Americans to accept. I think it was Howard Hendricks of Dallas Theological Seminary who said that many Americans get into a tizzie if they miss one section of a revolving door. Someone else has noted, "If today's average American is confronted with an hour of leisure, he is likely to palpitate with panic. An hour with nothing to do?...Everything has to be active and electric."

I repeat, how impatient we are. Time is passing and we want to make the most of it. We want to be like Christ NOW. We want to serve Him in a big way NOW. We want to fulfill our destiny NOW. We want our prayers answered NOW. Wait in submission for God to act in His own good time? It's almost asking too much, according to some of us.

I sense that too many women think they have to cram all their achieving into the second and third decades of their lives.

They're so afraid that life is getting away from them. Many go into a tailspin on their 30th birthday; they lament not having accomplished all they had hoped to by that advanced age.

We desperately need to understand that there really is enough time for what God wants us to do, for all that really needs to be done. Our times are in His hand. He orders our days. He chooses to lead us through various ages and stages according to His own timetable. If we have a Christian view of life, we will cooperate with His will for each season of our life, to learn in that season and to do in that season what is in line with His plan.

Colleen Townsend Evans, wife of Washington, D.C., pastor Louis Evans, expressed the idea this way: "This is a season in my life, it will not be forever. If I can submit to God in this season and do the things that He obviously has for me to do now, and not try to do all the things that belong in another season, I'm not only going to make it. But it's going to be a good season."

A writer-friend of mine says she sees her life as a book divided into chapters. She lived the chapter called childhood. The chapter entitled education. The one called career woman. The chapter of marriage, of parenting, of the empty nest, of part-time teaching and of ministry to couples. She is now writing the chapter called widow and ministry to the grieving.

Consider *your* life. What chapter are you writing at this point? Are you making it a good one? Are you impatient to be finished with it and onto the next? Are you resisting the lessons and growth of this stage? Or are you content in each season, knowing that the Lord is in control of your life and is working out His purpose in all you encounter?

Remember that Moses' life had many chapters and those chapters were divided into three parts. Each part lasted 40 years. God didn't hurry through any of those chapters or parts. Yet at every point, He was on time. He was never too early or too late.

## Nothing Wasted

Second, if we are to live fully, we must believe that God does not waste our time or experiences. Moses' years in the wilderness seemed to be a waste of the education he had received in the palace. In the final analysis, however, he needed both the palace years and the wilderness years before he was ready for the leadership years.

When I look back over my life, I can remember times when I felt that things I had learned were being wasted. At the advanced age of 40-plus, I realize that God knows I need time to experience in my life what I know in my head. It takes time and circumstances to make truth a practical, personal reality. One must live a little in order to add wisdom to knowledge.

About the time my children came along, I remember feeling that my outside ministry was being sidetracked. I felt strongly that I had to curtail my out-of-home activities to devote myself to full-time mothering. As I wiped noses and bottoms, I feared the world would go to perdition on skis while I was busy with kids. It seemed to me that life was passing me by, that my understanding of the Word and my desire to teach it was not finding a significant outlet to others except my family and the people who visited in our home.

One of my frustrations during my mother-of-small-children chapter was getting good time to study the Bible—a very common problem for mothers. In desperation during those years when Toby and Noelle were preschoolers, I began to write my devotions. I read a bit of Scripture and then noted what the passage said and what it meant and how it applied to practical, everyday living. If I got distracted by having to get a wee one a drink of water, I could come back to what I'd written and pick up my train of thought. In time, I amassed a stack of stenographer's notepads full of my times of reflection in the Word.

When my younger child had been in school a couple of years, I was asked to design a program for reading through the Bible and to write commentary to go along with each day's reading. It took me three years to complete that project, but I finally had written daily devotionals for a program of reading through the Bible in three years. And guess where I often turned to find insight on many Bible passages? The notebooks I had written in those years when my children were little, in those years when it felt as if I were on the shelf as far as significant ministry was concerned. In addition, my period of learning how to give selflessly to the needs of two small, demanding children proved to be character-building years.

If my speaking and writing ministry is practical and authentic today, it is due largely to God's past preparation of this instrument by means of a sickly childhood, adjusting to marriage, caring for stronged-willed children and more. The Lord has not wasted a single minute of my life, not even frustrations or disappointments or heartaches.

I hope you believe that God will not waste your time and your experiences. All you have lived through—the good, the bad, the indifferent—is a foundation for another phase of your growth and service.

## No Retirement Plan

Third, to live fully, we must know that God has no retirement plan. For as long as we live, we are meant to live as productively and creatively as He permits.

Think of it! Moses was fifteen years past the age of retirement when God called him to do what he had been born to do. My concern is that too many people retire from life and ministry just about the time they know enough about life to have something to offer others.

I've heard older women say they need to let younger women have the joy of ministry. They propose to get out of the way so younger women can pick up the reins of leadership. I agree with them. I think older women should train younger women in service and then give them ministry to do. But I don't think this justifies older women sitting in churches like so many dust-collecting museum pieces. My dear sisters, we give our ministries away again and again. But then we follow God's leading into other avenues of service He opens to us.

I believe strongly that God intends us to live until we die. I suspect that our most fruitful years in ministry may be in the last half of our lives. Bruce Larson said, "We're the ones who invented old age. We begin to be less creative, more cautious. We slow down at middle age and at 65 stop dead in our tracks and retire. I think God wants us to be a creative force for change at any age."[3]

I had the distinct privilege of knowing a lady named May Greene. She loved and served the Lord right up to the moment she went to heaven at age 91. For the last two years of her life, she was confined to a wheelchair due to the crippling affects of arthritis. But in her final 26 years, Sunday after Sunday, summer and winter, May taught a class of sixth graders.

She began that ministry when she was 65, retirement age. She loved her students and they loved her. In fact, parents lobbied the church to get their kids into her class. When I talked to her a few months before her death, she said she wasn't even thinking of quitting her responsibility because she believed the Lord had called her to that task. Sure enough, she didn't quit until she slept her way into God's presence one Saturday morning.

A couple of days ago I read the obituary of Herbert Lockyer in our local newspaper. At the age of 65, after a full life of preaching and teaching, he began writing. Between that time and his death at age 98 he penned more than 50 Christian books. Such examples humble me. I for one can't wait to see what I'm going to be when

I grow up. I fully expect that about the time I'm 60, I'm going to be a real dynamo in the cause of Christ. I may not be able to work harder due to decreased physical energy. But I believe I'll work more wisely and compassionately and confidently than I do now.

## Saying "Yes, God!" to Living

When was the last time you considered what you want to be when you grow up? You see, there never comes a time in our lives when we are free of the obligation to look up into the face of God and say, "Speak, Lord, for Thy servant is listening. What will You have me to do, Lord? Given the reality of my present circumstance, how can I best honor You?"

Saying, "Yes, God!" to living means perceiving and believing that all our days are to be lived to our Savior's glory and honor. It means trusting there is a purpose for our existence. It means accepting with grace each age and stage of our lives with their opportunities and limitations. It means not rushing ahead or lagging behind God's timetable for us. It means learning from our experiences as we go along. It means being ready to risk the changes the years impose. It means embracing new challenges until we die. It means singing with joyful confidence:

> My times are in Thy hand;
> My God, I wish them there;
> My life, my friends, my soul I leave
> Entirely to Thy care.[4]

"Lord, so teach us to number our days, that we may present to Thee a heart of wisdom" (Ps. 90:12).

## For Your Study

1. Like Moses, have you ever known God's will for you, but much time passed before you could do what He had asked you? If so, can you think of any lessons you learned during that interim period?

2. Can you recall certain periods of your life when you chafed under your circumstances? Felt time was passing you by? Thought God was wasting your talents in a desert place? From your present perspective, what are your perceptions about those times?

3. Are you now experiencing the thoughts and feelings mentioned in the previous question? From your reading about Moses, what facts can you hold on to that will help you through your situation?

4. How do you generally react to change? Can you remember—or are you presently—enduring miserable situations rather than risking making some needed changes in your life? Do you believe answers to some of your prayers may have been/are being delayed because you were/are not willing to accept God's answers?

5. What chapters have you already written in the book of your life? Do you think you wrote them well? What chapters are you now writing? Are you impatient in your present stage? Have you found, if you sidestepped certain lessons at one point in your life, that God later allowed circumstances to teach you what you had wanted to avoid? Are you growing wiser and better, as well as growing older?

6. What do you want to be when you grow up? What goals have you set for the future? How do you envision spending your retirement years? In what ways does your serving the Lord fit into those plans?

## Footnotes:

1. Catherine Marshall, *Something More* (New York: McGraw-Hill Book Co., 1974), p.5.
2. M. Blaine Smith, *One of a Kind* (Downers Grove, Ill.: InterVarsity Press, 1984), pp.57-8.
3. Bruce Larson, "Don't Do the Safe Thing," *Christian Herald*, June 1984, p.24.
4. "My Times Are in Thy Hand," by William F. Floyd (1791-1853).

# 2
## Hello, This Is God Calling

The Bible is full of incidents in which the Lord spoke to people. He talked to Noah. To Abraham, Isaac and Jacob. To the prophets. And to Paul. In the previous chapter we noted that He addressed Moses from the burning-but-not-burned-up bush. In these instances, often God's call was a commission to service; He requested that a certain task be performed.

Christian women today usually do not hear the audible voice of Jesus Christ. That does not mean He does not speak to them. He does. His message to them is in the Bible. They cannot escape the fact that His Word contains a mandate for ministry.

Jesus said He came to earth not to be served but to serve (Mt. 20:28). If we are His disciples, we will want to do as He did—serve the Father and His children. Indeed, if we love God with all our heart, soul, strength and mind, that love will compel us to be about His work in our world.

We naturally want to do for those we love. In fact, we find it incongruent even to imagine that we can say, "Yes, God!"

to living for Him without also saying, "Yes, God!" to laboring for Him. In a very practical sense, then, every believer has heard, "Hello, this is God calling. I have work for you to do."

That message came to Moses, and his response to it is most instructive for us. As we study the job interview recorded in Exodus 3:7-4:31, we discover some helpful insights into and answers for our concerns about our involvement in sacred business. So let's continue our look at the life of Moses.

When God told Moses he was to lead the Israelites out of Egyptian bondage, the man had no idea he was to become the greatest leader in the history of the Jewish people apart from their Messiah. We shall see that the whole idea of serving God by leading the Israelites to freedom absolutely boggled the shepherd's mind. So when the Lord said, "I will send you to Pharaoh so that you may bring My people...out of Egypt," Moses replied, "Who am I, that I should go to Pharaoh, and that I should bring the sons of Israel out of Egypt?" (3:10,11).

## Overwhelmed By Inadequacy

I suggest to you that we are seeing a very different Moses at age 80 than the man we saw at age forty. Earlier, he had been full of zeal and self-sufficiency. He had taken matters into his own hands in trying to right the wrongs done against his people by murdering an Egyptian. He had assumed his people would recognize his leadership skills and would flock to his and their common cause. But they didn't and they hadn't.

Consequently, Moses lived four decades with the knowledge he had not accomplished for the Israelites what he had hoped to. Surely he felt bitterly disappointed in himself—maybe even in God. For 40 years, the only practice he got in leadership was ruling over a bunch of dumb animals. He must have experienced great humiliation.

So, at the end of four decades, we find a man who felt totally inadequate. His years with his father-in-law had caused him to doubt the value of his education, his abilities and his political acumen. He certainly believed he had nothing to offer his people. Every moist shred of self-adequacy seems to have been leeched out of him by the dry hardship of desert living.

Thus, when God called him to serve Him, Moses' first response was to express his personal lack of fitness. In effect, he said, "Who me? You've got to be kidding! Who am I that I should go? I've been a simple shepherd for the past 40 years. I'm not special. What makes You think anybody will accept me? Will they really believe You want to use the likes of me?"

Moses' reaction was that of a person with low self-esteem. His response is typical of a person who has not realized his potential, who has felt thwarted in reaching his goals. He was like many whose education and talents, for whatever reasons, have not been discovered or have gone unused for a considerable period of time. As a result, Moses had come to underrate his abilities and to underrate God's desire and power to use him. His response may not have been so much that of a humble person but of one who doubts his worth and ability to serve God.

When I was a child I dedicated myself to God's service. As a result, I did what I knew to do to prepare for ministry. With all my heart, I desired and still want to be employed productively in the work of Christ's kingdom. I want to be a good and faithful servant of my Savior.

But, like Moses, I have wrestled with the thought that maybe I don't really have anything to offer the church. I have felt useless and, at times, doubted that God considers me usable. Frequently this has happened when certain doors of service closed to me, and I was experiencing a quiet Midian desert time in my life. Sometimes it has come about because I was overwhelmed by how far short I fall of perfect righteousness.

## Vulnerability Attacks

I confess I often have what I term vulnerability attacks before going to a speaking or teaching engagement. I sense my ordinariness so greatly I'm almost reluctant to get on the plane that will carry me to my destination. (What if the retreat committee decides I hadn't anything to say? Will they refuse to pay for my airline ticket?) I have no problem identifying with Moses' sense of unfitness at the age of eighty.

Maybe you don't either. More than anything else in the world, you want to serve the Lord. Yet you have a hard time believing He wants to and can do His work in and through you. Surely, if we are properly humble, we will know, as A.W. Tozer wrote, that "God does not need our help." But on the other hand, if we trust His Word, we will also know, as Tozer put it, "that the God who needs no one has in sovereign condescension stooped to work by and in and through His obedient children."[1]

Let's be realistic, Moses and you and I are incapable of serving God in and of ourselves. And the sooner we come to this conclusion the better. But we also need to understand that God can and does work through ordinary people like us. He takes a farm boy like Billy Graham and makes him the greatest evangelist of our time. He uses the foolish to confound the wise (1 Cor. 1:27). He permits you and me to help build His kingdom. This is the mystery of grace.

Now notice God's response to Moses' acknowledgement of inadequacy: "I will be with you" (3:12). Essentially, His answer to Moses' sense of unfitness was the promise of His presence. A nothing plus an Everything equals something extraordinary. God and Moses would make a majority. With God, nothing would be impossible.

I like also that the Lord said, "*When* you have brought the people out of Egypt, you shall worship God at this mountain." That's *when*, not *if*. There was no doubt about the outcome of the venture.

Moses was still not sure about the project. His first question, "Who am I?" was followed by a second: "Who are You?" Moses said to the Lord, "Behold, I am going to the sons of Israel, and I shall say to them, 'The God of your fathers has sent me to you.' Now they may say to me, 'What is His name?' What shall I say to them?'" (3:13).

Moses' second reaction concerned the character of God. He said, "If I tell the Hebrews God has sent me, they will ask which god? After all, Egyptians serve many idols; and I was brought up by polytheistic people. So they will say, 'You say God sent you but do you have any idea who God is? Can you tell us His name?'"

I'm not sure Moses was not acting like a person who goes to a psychiatrist and says, "I have a friend with a certain problem. What would you suggest she do about it?" In reality, the person speaking has the problem, but hopes to keep her privacy by pretending she's not involved. Perhaps Moses wanted to know about the God who was speaking to him. He wanted to find out, "Who are You? What is Your character? What do You do? What sort of God are You?"

We Christians often struggle with the same idea when called upon to serve Christ. We wonder if we really and truly have heard God's voice, or was it our imagination, or worse yet—the voice of Satan. We're afraid what we think is God's will for us may not be after all. We experience doubts about the nature of our Lord. And so we want to know, "What kind of God are You? Are You a God I can safely trust? What do You expect from me? What can I expect from You? Can I rely on Your name to accomplish Your work?"

To Moses' questions, the Lord said, "Tell them I AM has sent you. Tell them that the eternal, self-existent, unchangeable God has sent you. Tell them that the God who made a covenant with Abraham, Isaac and Jacob is going to act in keeping with His promise to them, the children of the patriarchs." And then the Lord spelled out what Moses was to do when he arrived in Egypt. God promised that the people would support Moses' leadership because it would be affirmed by the authority inherent in all that His name means and stands for (3:14-20).

## No Stingy God

Before we move on, I want to paraphrase what else God promised Moses (3:21,22): "The people will not go out empty, but full. They will not escape just by the skin of their teeth. They will not go out destitute to live in poverty in their new homeland. In essence, the Egyptians will pay them well for their years of servitude."

Those who act as if they serve a mean and stingy God need to focus on this tremendous thought. He is our extravagant Lord who feeds the multitude to the full and still has 12 baskets of food left over. How we need to rest in the promise that our Lord does exceeding abundantly beyond all that we are able to ask or even think (Eph. 3:29). He is not grudging in supplying us with what we need to be effective in His service.

As we go on, we find that Moses still was not convinced about the matter of his serving God and the people. He still had many what-ifs he wanted answers to. So he put forth a third question: "What if they will not believe me, or listen to what I say? For they may say, 'The Lord has not appeared to you'" (4:1). He simply repeated his fear of the people's unbelief. Ultimately, Moses wanted to know beforehand just what the results of his ministry would be.

The fact is, the Lord had already told him what he could expect. But that really shouldn't have been an issue anyway. The responsibility for results was not Moses' problem. Nevertheless, God graciously repeated His vow that He would produce miracles to confirm Moses' leadership, and He promised him divine power to validate and carry out his ministry (4:2-8).

As we consider this portion, we need to recognize that response and results are really not the main issue. It is enough for us that our Lord calls us. We obey Him and leave the consequences of our obedience with Him.

Moses still wasn't convinced. In Exodus 4:20 we discover that, because he was not the speaker type, he told God he could not serve Him. "I'm not the kind of person needed for this task," he declared. His claim of a lack of eloquence is especially interesting in light of Stephen's statement in Acts 7:22 that "he was a man of power in words." Remember, however, that for 40 years, his only addresses to a large group were aimed at sheep. In Moses' mind, I am sure, this hardly qualified as good practice of his oratorical skills.

## Anybody But Me, Lord

Some of us can identify with Moses' feeling that he lacked the necessary gifts for the job. Some of us, like him, are forever trying to enlighten the Omniscient. In essence, we tell the Perfect One He has made a mistake in choosing us to do a job.

I love God's reply to all this: "Who has made man's mouth? Go, and I will be with your mouth and will teach you want to say" (4:11,12). The principle here is that God's calling is God's enabling. The Creator is not powerless to make His instrument sufficient to the task.

The Lord will never ask His children to do what He does not equip them to do. If He directs one to minister, He will grant her the ability to minister and to accomplish what He wants to through her. And He will bring people alongside her to exercise their strong gifts in areas where she is weak.

After all this, look at Moses' final plea: "Please, Lord, now send the message by whomever Thou wilt" (4:13). Essentially, the man said, "Send somebody else. Anybody but me, Lord. I'd rather not do it, if it's all the same to You." In the final analysis, perhaps this was the primary reason Moses had kept sparring with God.

Ultimately, we will do what we want to do and try to get out of what we don't want to do. Haven't we said, "Here I am, God; send her! Let her do it. She would be so much better at this than I. Besides, that's not my cup of tea. I like my life as it is. What You're asking sounds like extra work and inconvenience."

When Moses expressed that attitude, God got angry with him. But even in His wrath, He met Moses where he was and promised him the comfort of his brother as a partner and colleague (4:14-17). I find it interesting that Moses took so much courage from this promise of support from another fallible human being. Yet he did not gather courage from the promise of the divine presence with him.

## No Sin Overlooked

And so Moses finally left Midian to travel to Egypt (4:18-20). On the way, a very frightening event occurred: "Now it came about at the lodging-place on the way that the Lord met him and sought to put him to death. Then Zipporah took a flint and cut off her son's foreskin and threw it at Moses' feet, and she said, 'You are a bridegroom of blood'—because of the circumcision" (4:24-26).

Do you find these verses a bit startling? After all, God had commissioned Moses and promised him he would lead the Hebrews out of Egypt. Now we find that the Lord threatened to kill His servant. What was going on?

Simply this: God had instituted circumcision as a sign of the covenant between Him and His people. About 500 years before,

He had told Abraham he and his male descendants were to carry on their body an indication of their special relationship with Him. Moses' parents had undoubtedly circumcised him, and he knew of the importance of that act. Yet he had failed to circumcise his son.

The Lord let Moses know He would not overlook this sin. He revealed to him that obeying God in one area does not excuse disobedience in another area. God showed him that a leader is not above divine law. In effect, the Lord told Moses he was expendable. The Hebrews would be delivered with or without Moses. Moses could have the honor and blessing of being God's instrument for their liberation. But he had to be a fit instrument or God would replace him.

How awesome it is for us to contemplate the fact that we can be busy, busy, busy with spiritual duties and yet not be pleasing to our Father. Our good deeds will not outweigh our refusal to deal with sin He has revealed to us. Apart from personal purity and obedience, our ministry has about as much lasting value as wood, hay and stubble (1 Cor. 3:12-15). And if we persist in preventing God's control in any area of our lives, He may set us aside and use another to carry on His work.

Perhaps because Moses was too ill to do so, his wife circumcised their son. Zipporah loved her husband enough that she didn't want him to die. But she was not above expressing her disgust for the bloody ritual his God imposed on them. Her action put Moses right with God. His life and his marvelous place in the scheme of divine history were not lost.

As Moses and his family traveled toward Egypt, God prepared Aaron's heart and those of the Hebrews to receive the deliverer. The people believed Moses was God's servant and worshiped the Lord (4:27-31).

## Confident of His Presence

Now let's gather together the thread of what we've studied and draw some lessons about serving Christ willingly and confidently. We've already mentioned that we often offer the same excuses Moses did when we hear God's call to ministry. We think we are personally and spiritually unfit. We don't think others will accept our calling to serve. We're afraid to risk failure and embarrassing results. We emphasize our lack of skills and gifts. We tell God to choose another since we'd rather not get involved.

But the call of God on our lives persists. He graciously extends the privilege of serving Him. He truly has no other plan for building His church except through people like us. And for every one of our excuses, He provides an answer, just as He did for Moses. If we accept His promises, we have no reason not to be about His work in our world. So let's deal one by one with Christ's assurances to us as we say, "Yes, God!" to ministry.

First, in our service we may be confident of the *divine presence*. For our difficulty in accepting the fact that the Lord can use the likes of us—common, ordinary people and sinners that we are—He has promised us, as He did Moses, His presence.

In Matthew 28:20 He said, "Lo, I am with you always." That promise follows hard on the heels of His command to go and make disciples of all nations. As somebody said, with the *go* comes the *lo*; as we set forth to serve, He walks alongside. Better than that, He is not only with us, but the Holy Spirit lives in us (Jn. 14:17).

We do not serve God because we deserve that high privilege. We have no goodness that makes us fit to do Christ's work. It is the perfect living Lord Himself in us that qualifies us to minister in His name.

Some of the most obnoxious church workers I have met are those whose confidence is in themselves. They act full of self-importance. On the other hand, one of the greatest detriments to the church is a lack of solid self-esteem based squarely on Scripture. Inferior-feeling women fail to serve because they don't trust the sufficiency of God in their lives. When all is said and done, the woman who knows she is nothing—but in Christ is all she needs to be—will serve effectively and confidently.

## Confidence in His Name

Second, in our service we may be confident in the *divine name*. Who has asked us to serve? The eternal I AM. For our concern about whether or not we have really heard the voice of God or whether or not we have really determined the will of God correctly, we have the promise of the Scripture: The Lord has made His name known to us and in His name we can know His will.

Someday, I would like to do a series of messages on the names of God. At this point, I can only touch on the topic ever so briefly. But I can say this: God's name tells you not only *who* He is but *what* He is. Warren Wiersbe put it this way: "Every name that He wears is a blessing that He shares."[2] Only as we study the Word will we learn His name; that is, will we come to know the kind of God we serve.

The more we know what kind of God we serve, the better we'll be able to determine what His will is for us. The more we know what kind of God we serve, the better we'll know how greatly we can trust Him. The more we know what kind of God we serve, the better we'll know what He expects of us.

He says to us today, "I AM has sent you. You can serve Me confidently because I *am* your wisdom. I *am* your strength. I *am* your guide. I *am* your love. I *am* your sufficiency. Whatever it is you need Me to be, you fill in the blank. I *am* your ____. I AM is sending you. So whatever you say or do, you can say or do it in My name (Col. 3:17). I am the kind of God who responds to those who ask in My name" (Jn. 16:23).

I tell you, it gives me courage to serve the Lord when I know He is with me. And knowing Him as my I AM makes me even bolder. He is the kind of God who gives me a sense of authority as I minister in His name.

## Confident of His Power

Third, in our service we may be confident of *divine power*. Jesus said, "All authority in heaven and on earth has been given to me. Go..." (Matt. 28:18,19). When we get overly concerned, as Moses was, about the results of our service, we need to understand that God has all authority; He is omnipotent—He cannot fail. He is the Lord God Almighty. He has all the might He needs to accomplish His will through us. And He has promised His power to those of us upon whom the Holy Spirit has come (Acts 1:8).

We may not see fantastic response to our ministry, but that is not because we or our Father lack power. We serve Christ in the power of the Holy Spirit, and we are content to leave the results to Him. The important thing is that God has called us; He has empowered us; and we have been obedient. We may not look really productive. We may not get written up in *Today's Christian Woman*. But still we trust that the power of God is at work in us. In spite of the apparent effectiveness or ineffectiveness of our service, we are confident of God's power. Behind the scenes of our ministry, He is subtly and potently accomplishing His will.

## Confident of Our Giftedness

Fourth, in our service, we may be confident of our *divine giftedness*. When we are tempted as Moses was to beg off doing what God asks us to do because we think we don't have the necessary skills, we must trust that when God calls us He enables us.

In our previous study of Moses' life, we said there was no Israelite more eminently qualified to lead his people than Moses. But time and again, he kept yammering that he wasn't eloquent. Perhaps he didn't need eloquence. Or maybe God intended to make him the speaker type. But Moses never found out, because initially he did not believe God would grant him the ability to do what he had been asked to do. He never found out because he argued until he was given Aaron as a spokesman.

The New Testament speaks clearly of the fact that each Christian is a gifted person. The Lord has called every person to serve Him, and He has equipped each one to minister uniquely in His church. He doesn't give us a task and then a pat on the back for good luck. He has fitted us for the role He has chosen for us in the body.

In the confines of this chapter, I cannot discuss your giftedness. I ask you to consider 1 Corinthians 12, Romans 12, Ephesians 4 and 1 Peter at your convenience. On the basis of these passages, I assure you that you do have ability to serve Christ well. I pray that you are confident He has equipped you for the ministry to which He has called you.[3]

I am so glad we are alive right now. I know of no other time in the history of Christianity with more possibilities and potential for women in ministry. It is a great day to serve Christ and His church. Oh, let's not ignore our opportunity. My fellow servants of Jesus Christ, let's respond positively to the challenge of God's call to live and labor for Him.

It's our decision. We have a choice. We can sit on the sidelines and offer excuses for our lack of involvement in the work of the Kingdom. Or we can move into the action with confidence that the Lord of the harvest has called us forth as reapers. He has sent us forth with His presence, with His name, with His power and with His gifts. So in your mind's eye, picture this conversation:

## A Person-to-Person Call

"Hello, this is God calling. I have a job for you. You'll not find any labor more worthwhile and fulfilling than what I offer. I'll provide you with everything you need for the task. The compensation and benefits are great. And the retirement home for My employees is unlike anything you can imagine."

"Lord, I'm so glad You called. I'd count it an honor and a privilege to work for You. Just say what, when and where, and I'll be there. It is my intention never to resign or retire from Your service. I make this commitment simply because I know I can trust You."

## For Your Study

1.   Of all the excuses Moses gave to God for not wanting to lead the Israelites, with which do you most identify and why?

2.   What are the promises God gave to Moses and has given to you to bolster your confidence to step out in ministry?

3.   In the light of these promises, do you need to confess an area of unbelief—a point at which you are not trusting God so that you are not so involved as you ought to be in serving Him? If so, remember the promise of 1 John 1:9 as you confess your sin.

4.   Read 1 Corinthians 1:26-29. What do these verses say to you about having to possess great abilities to do God's work? Do you think personal inadequacy can be beneficial in ministry? Why?

5.   Can you think of some personal examples of God's calling you to do what you felt ill-equipped to do? Did you discover His enabling as you faithfully tried to do what He asked of you? Share this with others for their good and God's glory.

6. What do you feel is lacking today in your life and witness? What do you need God to be to you? Remember, He is your I AM. You fill in the blanks:

I am your_____

I am your_____

I am your_____

I am your_____

Footnotes:

1. A.W. Tozer, *The Knowledge of the Holy* (Harrisburg, Penn.: Christian Publications, Inc., 1961) p. 43.

2. Warren Wiersbe, *The Wonderful Names of Jesus* (Lincoln, Neb.: Back to the Bible, 1980), p.5.

3. For more on spiritual gifts see *Yes, God...I Am a Creative Woman*, edited by Dorothy Dahlman, and *The Ministering Woman*, by Pamela Heim, Harvest Publications, Arlington Heights, Ill.

# 3
# *If at First You Don't Succeed*

If at first you don't succeed, you're about average. And that's not all bad. In fact, failing can be wonderfully positive. Having said that, I don't deny we would rather experience the thrill of victory as opposed to the agony of defeat.

That's why seminars on successful living abound. Do you want to succeed in marriage, in real estate, in being assertive, in gourmet cooking or whatever? Then just pay your money and listen to the experts. Do you want to learn how those who made it to the top got there? You need look no further than your newsstand or bookstore; the inside story is right there in black and white.

This chapter has something to say about success, but it also deals with failure. Let's face it! Most of us have had lots of experience with defeat. We don't particularly enjoy it; certainly we don't go looking for it. But it is a fact of life. We do well, therefore, to learn how to deal with failure successfully and with a sense of hope. In a very real sense, we can't say, "Yes, God!" to living unless we are willing to accept losing as well as winning.

Again we are going to turn our attention to Moses as we study success and failure. We rather quickly passed over his failure to assume leadership of the Israelites when he was forty. Remember, he had decided to identify with the Hebrews rather than take his place in Pharaoh's court. In Exodus 2:11-15 we read that he was enraged at the injustice the Egyptians were inflicting on the Israelites. So, he killed an Egyptian who had been beating a Hebrew.

If Moses had expected that act to catapult him into leadership among his people, he must have been sorely disappointed. Not only did the Israelites not acclaim him as their liberator. But he found himself forced into exile in Midian. Undoubtedly, he had failed to unite his people and rally them to the cause of their independence.

But 40 years later, Moses stood on the brink of success. God met him in the incident of the burning-but-not-burned-up bush and promised him that he would lead his people out of Egypt. If we expected Moses to say, "Good deal. I've been waiting for this chance for 40 years," then we will be surprised. Actually, as we saw in the last chapter, he gave a number of excuses why he could not accomplish what God had asked him to do.

One of Moses' concerns had to do with his fear of failure. He had failed once to elicit his people's support for his leadership and liberation of them. That previous defeat still rankled 40 years later. He struggled with the idea of risking failure a second time.

Finally, however, Moses went to Egypt to begin the process of freeing the Hebrews. Right off the bat, Aaron believed God had called his brother to liberate the people. And initially the people worshiped God for sending Moses as their deliverer.

Now let's take up the narrative where we left off in the last chapter. Look at Moses' first interview with Pharaoh in Exodus 5:1-14. Moses asked the ruler to let the Hebrews go. And Pharaoh said, "NO!" In my book, that was not an auspicious start.

Furthermore, the stubborn Egyptian leader said the Israelites evidently were not working hard enough if they had time to think about anything other than their jobs. As a result, he made their labor even harder. Any way you look at it, Moses failed in his first meeting with Pharaoh. He not only failed to secure the release of the Hebrews slaves, but made their situation worse.

I have stated that Moses failed, and in one sense he surely did. But in another sense, we might say he succeeded. It all depends on your definition of success.

Dr. Howard Hendricks states: "Success is always related to the will of God. Daniel was in the lions' den in the will of God. To the Christian, there is no success outside the will of God, and there is nothing but success in the will of God."

## The Hall of Famous Faithful

With this in mind, consider some people the Bible describes as successful. In Hebrews 11, we discover many of them. Quite honestly, those God listed in this Hall of Famous Faithful were not what you and I would call wildly successful by any normal standard. They didn't do anything particularly spectacular.

For example, Abraham received praise because he moved to an alien land at the Lord's command. Sarah's big success was to give birth to a baby. Joseph ranked high for believing that the day would come when his people would leave Egypt and resettle in Canaan. Rahab gained her place among the successful faithful for hiding spies in her house. And get this: many were considered successful because they were tortured, mocked, scourged, imprisoned and killed. In the natural that surely sounds like failure, does it not?

## When Are We Successful?

In Romans 8:37 Paul assures believers that they overwhelmingly conquer. One sees a picture of Christians parading as extraordinary victors. But it is interesting to note that the apostle speaks of great winners. Yet at the same time he says believers experience tribulation, distress, persecution, famine, nakedness, peril and sword (Rom. 8:35). It would seem we need to reconsider the meaning of success.

An article by Dr. Vernon Grounds really stirred me about this matter of success. He stated that God sometimes calls people to "tedious mediocrity" as the world judges it. He wrote, "Regardless, God's approval is the most important point. It is far more important to follow God's blueprint for your life than to be another Billy Graham or Hal Lindsey or Robert Schuller or Bill Bright."[1] As women we might say, "It is far better for you to obey God's leading in your life than to be another Catherine Marshall or Joyce Landorf or Mother Teresa."

Again, when are we successful? *We are succesful when we are steadily becoming the unique person God intends us to become and when we are doing what He asks us to do.*

By this definition, the prophets of Israel were personally successful from the divine perspective. Surely they failed to call the people back to God. The Jews did not repent in the centuries when the messengers warned the kingdoms of Judah and Israel of coming punishment. Nevertheless, the prophets faithfully declared God's Word as they had been commanded to do. With them as with Moses, the responsibility for success or failure was really God's problem. But in the natural, we can say they failed to accomplish what they tried to do.

Let's move on in our consideration of Moses.

## Losing Some Battles

As we noted, Pharaoh decided to work the Hebrews even harder. The slaves sought mercy from the ruler; but hardhearted to their distress, he accused the Israelites of being lazy, very lazy. He refused to give them the necessary supplies to make bricks. Yet he also continued to expect the full quota of bricks to be made (5:15-19).

At that, the Israelites turned on Moses and Aaron. They said to the two men, "May the Lord look upon you and judge you, for you have made us odious in Pharaoh's sight and in the sight of his servants, to put a sword in their hand to kill us" (5:21). They charged that Moses and Aaron would be the death of them.

That incident is marvelously instructive to us. We learn that we can do God's will and everything may still seem to go wrong. Moses did what the Lord told him to when he asked Pharaoh to let the people go. The man refused. Moses did right in seeking his people's freedom. But the Israelite foremen turned against God's appointed leaders nevertheless.

You see, the Lord does not always work things out as we anticipate He will. Sometimes you and I have set out with such high hopes to live the Christian life and serve the Lord. And we have run into one brick wall after another. Perhaps some of the biggest barriers have been thrown up by fellow Christians. It's our brothers and sisters in Christ who have discouraged us most in what we believe God has asked us to do. Often when this happens, we begin to question: Did we misread God's will? Where did we go wrong? Is the Lord playing games with us?

Jeremiah experienced this. When the people refused to heed his prophecies, he said, "O Lord, Thou hast deceived me and I was deceived....I have become a laughingstock all day long; everyone mocks me....for me the word of the Lord has resulted in reproach and derision all day long. But if I say, 'I will not remember Him or speak any more in His name,' then in my heart it becomes like a burning fire shut up in my bones; and I am weary of holding it in, and I cannot endure it'' (Jer. 20:7-9).

You and I need to grasp the fact that we obey Christ because His love compels us to follow His leading. And if in obeying Him the way gets rough, that is not a sure indication we are out of His will.

Mary, the mother of Jesus, gives us beautiful insights into this truth. Mary was certainly in the will of God when she gave Him her body to produce Jesus. In fact, due to the nature of the virgin birth it would be illogical to question whether Mary was in the will of God to bear Christ. Yet her life was one heartbreak after another.

I don't suppose Mary's pregnancy was any more of a picnic for her than it is for most women. She may have felt the misery of heartburn, nausea, leg cramps, shortness of breath, awkwardness and the like. Worse yet, she was pregnant on her wedding day and people never let her forget it. Three decades later, folks threw up in Jesus' face their doubts about His paternity.

Mary had to travel more than 35 miles either by donkey or on foot in the last stage of her pregnancy. She delivered in a strange place, maybe without any female relatives to aid her. She had no privacy following the birth, for a bunch of illiterate, perhaps sheep-smelly, strangers trooped into the room to see her Son.

Mary didn't have money to ease her way either. She was a poor lady. She offered the smallest offering for her purification—two doves. While Jesus was still small, she was forced to travel to a foreign country just to save His life. Nevertheless, she knew many a mother's son was killed because of her Son. And she must have grieved deeply over that horrible fact. Perhaps some were her friends' baby boys.

The children Mary had never really accepted or believed in their Brother during His ministry. Truly, His mother did not fully understand her Son at twelve or even afterward. There's a strong possibility she was widowed before her children were grown. If so, she faced the problems of a single parent.

Finally, Mary saw Jesus—the will of God for her—rejected, mocked, defamed, tortured and killed. That must have seemed like the failure of failures to her. Certainly, Mary shows us that a smooth life is not proof one is within the will of God.

F.B. Meyer noted, "When Jesus died, failure seemed written across His life-work. A timid handful of disciples was all that remained...and they seemed disposed to go back to their fishing boats. Man despised Him....But that very cross...deemed His supreme disgrace and dethronement, has become the steppingstone of universal dominion."

Will you grasp this? Sometimes it is within the Master's plan that His children lose some battles in the course of winning the war. So it was that an obedient Moses experienced failure.

## Misplaced Confidence

Sadly, Moses' failure led to his discouragement and even greater sense of his inadequacy for the job God had called him to do (5:22,23). But let's admit it. Often our defeats and troubles also cause us depression, bitterness, resentment, doubt and more.

Sometimes when we determine to walk more closely with the Lord, or we launch out in Christian ministry, we consciously or unconsciously think we possess some ability to live right or serve well. Oh, we would deny it and piously say, "Only the Lord can accomplish this." But, in reality, the self-pity and the self-blame we engage in when we fail indicate that our confidence was in ourselves. If all along we truly accepted our inadequacy and believed the battle is the Lord's (1 Sam. 17:47), I don't think we would become so easily discouraged.

Now note God's response to Moses' distress: "I am the Lord....Say to the sons of Israel, 'I am the Lord and I will bring you out from under the burdens of the Egyptians, and I will deliver you from their bondage. I will also redeem you with an outstretched arm and with great judgments. Then I will take you for My people, and I will be your God; and you shall know that I am the Lord your God, who brought you out from under the burdens of the Egyptians. And I will bring you the land which I swore to give to Abraham, Isaac, and Jacob, and I will give it to you for a possession; I am the Lord.''' (6:2-8).

Mark the use of the word *I* in that passage. I am the Lord. I will bring you out. I THE LORD! This is MY problem. God didn't want Moses to be confused about who was in charge.

And the Lord did not intend to succeed just somehow, but totally and stupendously. God planned to win with a flourish.

After that, Moses went back to talk to the people; but the despondent folks didn't listen to him (6:9). And Moses still thought it was all his fault. In Exodus 6:12 Moses said the trouble was that he was not the speaker type. Imagine it! He thought God's tremendous plan for the liberation of millions rested on his way with words! He didn't have a clue that his failure was all a part of God's grand design.

It was quite a while before Pharaoh literally commanded the people to get out of his sight and out of his land. Ten plagues were sent on Egypt before that time. Each of nine plagues represented one failure after another. Nine times a stubborn ruler failed to be convinced about letting the Hebrews go. At the same time, each plague gave increasing evidence of the power of the Lord God Almighty.

## God Permits Failure

Now let's stop here and gather together some thoughts on what it means to view failure with expectancy. How can we experience a sense of hope when faced with what seems like defeat? Can we look at apparent loss creatively so that we are willing to risk again, that is, to keep on living to the full? Yes. Yes. Yes. First, we must believe God permits failure to be a part of life. God does not erase all possibility of defeat when we become Christians. In the world we will have tribulation (Jn. 16:33). The rain of affliction will fall on us just folks as much as on the unjust. We will not succeed as the world judges success in everything we do. In fact, the Lord in His love will permit failure to come our way.

Let's be honest, it's tough to accept the fact that a loving Lord sometimes permits difficult things in our lives. We wonder how a loving God can allow us to be touched by failure, loss, death, illness, poverty and so on. Harder yet is the command of 1 Thessalonians 5:18 to give thanks in all those things, or the command of Ephesians 5:20 to give thanks always for everything. We can understand praising His name in the good times; but in the bad times, must we do the same?

Hannah Whitall Smith wrote in *The Christian's Secret of a Happy Life*: "What is needed...is to see God in everything and to receive everything directly from His hands, with no intervention of second causes....To the child of God, everything comes directly from their Father's hands, no matter who or what may have been the apparent agents. There are no 'second causes' for them. Second causes must all be under the control of our Father, and not one of them can touch us except with His knowledge and by His permission.

"It may be the sin of man that originates the action, and therefore the thing itself cannot be said to be the will of God; but by the time it reaches us it has become God's will for us, and must be accepted as directly from His hands. No man or company of men, no power in earth or heaven, can touch that soul which is abiding in Christ, without first passing through His encircling presence, and receiving the seal of His permission....Nothing can disturb or harm us, except He shall see that it is best for us, and shall stand aside to let it pass."[2]

## Blowing it Badly

Second, we must expect God to instruct us through failure. Blowing it badly can be wonderfully enlightening. Failure goes a long way in destroying a spiritually adolescent know-it-all attitude.

I have heard single people speak with great conviction about how marriages ought to be. I have heard people who aren't parents argue that they have the formula for rearing children who won't rebel. I have heard the healthy and the skinny and the optimistic pontificate at length about how to deal with sickness, overweight and depression. I have listened to many a dogmatic Christian talk as if she had tied up the whole ball of biblical wisdom into one neat package. And she didn't take kindly any disagreement with her point of view.

A while back I talked to a woman who told me she does everything the Bible tells her to do. (I'm not kidding!) She said that when believers trust and obey God everything will just fall into place for them. As an example, she said she had prayed for her adult children's conversions. And each of them had accepted Jesus Christ as Savior in a very short time. In her opinion, that is the normal Christian life. I might say she is a relatively new Christian who apparently has fallen into the name-it-and-claim-it wing of the church.

I didn't bother to dispute with her. If I had told her of my failures and of the delays of success I've experienced, I'm sure she would have attributed them to my sin and unbelief. Like Job's comforters, she would have declared that only unfaithful children of God face defeat.

I know Christ loves that woman; therefore, I believe He is going to allow some failures and disappointments in her life. And when that happens, she can do one of three things. She can deny reality and say what has happened has not happened. Or she can stubbornly hold on to her ideas that God will do anything she wants Him to do if only she will trust and obey Him better. Or, if she's open to it, she can learn from the situation a bit more of who God is and who she is. She can learn that God is not her puppet, that she is fallible and that she as a human being is going to feel the negative impact of living in a fallen world.

I personally have found that experiencing failure has given me a better understanding of the kind of woman I am. When things are going well, it is easy for me to gloss over my weaknessess. When life is smooth, it's not hard to pretend I'm A-OK. But when I feel defeated, I have been forced to search my heart and deal more honestly with myself.

Failure has also driven me to the Word and to prayer, to learn more about the kind of God I serve and how I might expect Him to operate. Disappointments have forced me to wrestle with the truth that I can never fully figure God out and that I cannot put Him in a box. Hard times have made me realize I should not even pretend to know all His reasons for allowing me to go through what I go through. Frustrations cause me to trust Him even when I don't understand. Elusive success forces me to live by faith and not by sight.

I don't have a Bible verse to back this up. But my experience leads me to believe that almost every worthwhile thing I have learned about spiritual living has resulted from failure and trouble. In fact, I think I could not have learned certain lessons except through experiencing pain and defeat. I am talking about vital, experiential heart knowledge here and not mere impersonal, intellectual facts. The first kind is the stuff of spiritual life and growth.

As I said, some things can only be learned through time and experience. I'm not particularly happy with that idea, but that's the way it has been for me and for other Christians I know.

I can't help but think of Joni Eareckson Tada. What a wealth of understanding she has gained by sitting in a wheelchair. And I have been blessed by the insights Corrie ten Boom learned in a concentration camp. Catherine Marshall's bout with tuberculosis gave her wisdom that has ministered to me as I've read her books.

Nevertheless, what these godly women have said to me becomes real only when I wrestle with my own problems.

I hope you are not discouraged by the idea that God often uses pain to shape His children. I'm not. Because I believe failure teaches me, I'm getting better and better at welcoming defeat and hurt as friends. As James 1:3 commands, I am more inclined now than I used to be to rejoice in brick walls. I want to learn the lessons the hard school of trial will teach me.

## Humbled, Not Crushed

Third, we must realize that God permits failure to humble us. Moses' failures stripped away every sense of his own adequacy until he was aware of his total inability to accomplish anything of worth for the Lord. Whereas at one time he felt confident that he could bring about justice for his people, he later knew he was not up to the task. His experience of failure made the difference.

The apostle Peter was just as sure he was a true blue disciple of Jesus. He felt certain he would be willing to fight and die for his Friend. He knew he would never turn his back on Him. But after denying Christ three times, he was stripped of his sense of personal goodness and loyalty.

Afterward, when Jesus asked Peter, "Do you love me?" the man made no exaggerated claims about his affection for his Master. He said, "Lord, I don't know myself. I do know I can't trust myself to do the right thing. You know me, and only You know who and what I am (Jn. 21:15-17). That's humility. And he learned it through failure. It gave him a true perspective of himself. It revealed his inadequacy. It pointed out his need to rely totally on the Lord if he was to be or do anything of value.

God will not share His glory with another. He will engineer situations to point out that the issue is not what we can do for Him. The issue is the absolute necessity of knowing who He is and that every good thing in us is from Him. He will allow us to try in our own strength, cleverness and skill to live godly lives and to serve Him; and He will let us fail miserably. When we have been thoroughly humbled, when we have a sure sense of our insufficiency, then He can live in us and use us. Then we will set out to live for and serve Him with total reliance on His sufficiency and enabling. And He will get all the honor and praise if people see us as successes. But if it should appear that we have failed, we will not be crushed, because we trust the results to Him.

## Turning Around Failure

Fourth, we must recognize the fact that God permits failure to soften us. Defeat makes us sympathetic with the weaknesses of others. It destroys our superior, judgmental spirit.

Nobody can comfort the woman with an unfaithful husband like a woman who has an adulterous spouse. Nobody understands the hurt of a parent with a wayward child like another rejected parent. Nobody is more tender with the sinner than the one who knows the depths of her own sin and God's forgiveness. Only those who realize the strength of temptation can restore the trespasser in a spirit of gentleness as Galatians 6:1 commands.

You see, our failures help us identify with others' failings. When I counsel, I am not easily shocked by the problems of women. I only have to look within myself to know I am capable of their lapses. My personal defeats have taught me how to love other people as full of faults as myself. I know that because I have struggled and sometimes blown it as a Christian, as a wife, as a mother, I have insight into and compassion for the struggles of my sisters in Christ.

By the same token, our failures help other failing people identify with us. In my speaking ministries, I have talked about the problems I have had with a husband who had difficulty communicating. I have discussed my struggles in mothering an emotionally disturbed child. I have admitted my inability to love an unlovely person. Because of my willingness to share these painful experiences, others feel safe in approaching me. They expect me to understand their weaknesses and not condemn them. They find encouragement that God by His grace can and has turned around my failure to work for good in my life, as Romans 8:28 promises.

When our son Toby was about six years old, my husband Lowell and I were remodeling our kitchen. At the end of one strenuous day, I was tired and cranky and Toby was feeling ornery. He disobeyed me. I yelled at him and he yelled right back. Lowell was standing nearby and gave Toby a swat on the bottom for sassing me. Toby dissolved in tears. And I started to cry. I knew I had failed to deal with my son in a Christlike manner.

I confessed my sin to the Lord and then I went to talk to Toby. I told him I was wrong in raising my voice at him. I explained it was my conviction that I should not have disciplined him in anger. I asked his forgiveness and assured him of my love.

Toby in turn asked me to forgive his failure to obey me. As he sat on my lap in the rocking chair that evening, he began to ask questions more profound than most adults have asked. Why do we do wrong when we want to do right? he wanted to know. How can we overcome those old sin natures which trip us up spiritually? It was a moving time of explaining spiritual truth to my little guy. And it all began with failure—his to obey and mine in shouting my indignation.

I don't condone sin. I wish I never failed God. But I have discovered He can even use spiritual defeats to bless me. Consequently, I can face failure with joyful hope. And so can you if you will allow failure to instruct you, to humble you and to soften you.

I delight in these words from Catherine Marshall: "The Gospel truly is good news. The news is that there is no situation—no breakage, no loss, no grief, no sin, no mess (no failure)—so dreadful that out of it God cannot bring good, total good, not just 'spiritual' good, if we allow Him to. Our God is the Divine Alchemist. He can take the junk from the rubbish heap of life, and melting this base refuse in the pure fire of His love, hand us back—gold."[3]

## For Your Study

1. Read Hebrews 11. From what you learned in past study, list the failures and trials of the people mentioned in that passage. Why do you think God included them in His record of the faithful?

2. Contrast the world's standard of success against God's standard. In what ways do you think the church gets into difficulty when it measures spiritual ministries against the secular yardstick of success?

3. What are the dangers in assuming that problems indicate one is outside the Lord's will?

4. Have you found that the brick walls you run into as you try to minister often are built by fellow Christians? What is the biblical response when faced with this kind of discouragement and opposition? Are you an encourager or discourager to the workers in your church?

5. Meditate at length on the idea that discouragement in ministry often finds its roots in having relied on self rather than on God. How would leaving the results to the Lord prevent discouragement?

6. Recall some failures in your life. Did you allow God to turn the garbage into gold by gaining instruction, humility and com-

passion from those situations? Have you personally experienced the truths of Romans 5:3-5 and James 1:2-4? Have you passed on to others what you've gained according to the model found in 2 Corinthians 1:3-4?

Footnotes:

1. Vernon Grounds, "Faith to Face Failure, Or What's So Great About Success?" *Christianity Today*, Dec. 9, 1977, p.13.

2. Hannah Whitall Smith, *The Christian's Secret of a Happy Life* (New Jersey: Fleming H. Revell Co., 1952), p. 144-46.

3. Catherine Marshall, *Something More* (New York: McGraw-Hill Book Co., 1974, ), p.7.

# PART III:
# SAYING ''YES, GOD''
# TO MINISTRY

## By Roberta Collins

# 1
# *A Look In The Mirror*

A Jonathan and David poster hangs inside my kitchen cupboard with this reminder:

> When in the mirror of His love
> I look at my reflection,
> I accept myself for who I am—
> With all my imperfection.[1]

Have you ever suddenly glanced at your reflection in a store window? When I have, I usually wish I hadn't. As my father says about himself, "I never quite present the dashing figure I had in mind." Most of us avoid looking at ourselves too closely. Our imperfections are too painful to confront. And yet, as my kitchen poster reminds me, in the mirror of Christ's love, we can dare to see ourselves.

We need to look frequently—to take the risk of seeing ourselves honestly—through the mirror of God's Word. There we see who we are and much more. Who we can become is promised. As William Barclay says, God's knowledge of us holds "a purpose and a plan and a design and a task."[2] Come look! is God's offer. Accepting the possibility of all we can be is the beginning of ministry.

## More Than A Cosmetic Change

I'm one of those unfortunate people who always gets "scared fat." I wish I could get scared skinny. Just once. When my husband Howard felt called to the pastoral ministry some years ago, I accepted with all my heart what this would mean to our family. But I had never been a pastor's wife. She's perfect, you know. I'm not. And I was scared.

Sure enough! In the next three years I gained weight...never mind how much!

One morning while studying my Bible, my eyes fell on Romans 12:1 and 2: "I appeal to you therefore, brethren, and beg of you in view of (all) the mercies of God, to make a decisive dedication of your bodies—presenting all your members and faculties—as a living sacrifice, holy (devoted, consecrated) and well pleasing to God, which is your reasonable (rational, intelligent) service and spiritual worship. Do not be conformed to this world...but be transformed (changed) by the (entire) renewal of your minds— by its new ideals and its new attitude—so that you may prove (for yourselves) what is the good and acceptable and perfect will of God...."

These verses were asking me to dedicate my physical body to God. More startling than this, my service and worship were required. For the first time, I dared to look at what fear had done to me physically. I had been scared fat. Hardly an ego builder. I knew God wanted me to be emotionally and physically healthy. And more than a cosmetic change was needed.

Immediately I signed up at a health spa, found two friends to go with me, and bought some brown leotards. I looked like a plumped up raisin as I stood before the instructor in my spa outfit. First she evaluated me. (My own estimate had been kind.) Then, based on reality, we set a goal and she designed a program for me.

The rest was up to me. All the evaluation and programing in the world wouldn't work unless I worked. And work I did. The instructor guided me. My friends encouraged. But actually changing was my responsibility. It was personal discipline time.

## A Welcome Communication

The process that got me back in shape physically is similar to the process of becoming an effective minister. First, you must look at who you are without God. Then you must look at His plans. Sadly, for many people much of their potential lies unread in His Word. Or it is read but unheeded. God waits to hear you say: "Lord, there is more to life than I'm living. Show me who You are. Show me my place in your plans. I want to change."

Regardless of what brings you to this welcome communication—whether failure, ineptness, incompleteness— God hears your plea and accepts you with open arms. The process of change begins with your plea. The mystery is that in knowing Him you find the significant you.

Unfortunately, in the softness of today's living, we water down the meaning of knowing God. We treat the topic as if it were a social engagement or a stimulating exchange of ideas. Yet much more is involved. Books on self-improvement, on ministry skills, and on the importance of personhood bow before who God is.

The Old Testament use of the word "know" means intimacy. Abraham knew his wife Sarah—experiencing physical intimacy and sharing the deepest possible expression of human love and giving. To know God is to experience this same level of intimacy mentally, emotionally and spiritually. Our continuing intimate relationship with Him brings the security, purpose and value that we lack. And these are springboards for becoming adequate ministers.

Wouldn't it be nice if all that was required to know God intimately was as simple as an occasional trip to the beauty shop? You could just sit in your chair and let Him change you.

We could set appointments for improvement treatments whenever it seemed convenient. "Put me down for a Thursday in two months. I plan to enjoy some camping this summer...won't be around much...my parents are coming...I should be free by September."

## No Shortcuts

How we wish for a shortcut that could bring permanent results. If only some experience or doctrine could instantly produce lasting maturity and the ability to minister. But there is none. Instead, we are offered a beginning, a continuing in the way and, finally, promised results.

Using the Word of God as a mirror, we must look at ourselves in light of His plan for us as ministers. His evaluation is fair. His advice works. Then with our personal discipline and commitment to change, the Holy Spirit can begin to transform us bit by bit.

The principle is seen in 2 Corinthians 3:18 : "And all of us, as with unveiled face, (because we) continued to behold (in the Word of God) as in a mirror the glory of the Lord, are constantly being transfigured into His *very own* image in ever increasing splendor *and* from one degree of glory to another; (for this comes) from the Lord (Who is) the Spirit."

This is not the same transformation that happens at salvation when we become new creations in Him. This is a continuing transforming process that causes us to become more and more like God in attitude and conduct. Our transformation occurs as we grow in our knowledge of our Lord. Consistent study, meditation and prayer are the tools. Gradually we change.

## Motivated to Minister

When we consistently seek to know God intimately, two things happen: 1) we are motivated to minister; and 2) our growth brings increased ability to serve. Think for a moment of our world. If you were asked what motivates most people to work and contribute, what would you say? No doubt you would think of the self-centered big three: power, money and recognition—the world's value system.

You must have *power*. If you don't, someone else will control you, use you, hurt you. All of us want to be in charge of our own lives.

You must have *money*. How else can you have all you want, influence others, gain control?

You must have *recognition*. Humans have a basic need to be accepted and admired. No one wants to be called a "nobody."

Some years ago, from a secure place on a bank high above Niagara Falls I watched a powerful whirlpool that swirled downstream. Everything near the pool was being sucked into its center and down. The world's value system is like this. You're drifting along when suddenly it catches you. You're helpless. The system's influence is powerful!

The wisest man in Scripture, Solomon, was caught by its undertow. When he began his search for happiness, he looked for it in power, money and recognition. In Ecclesiastes, he warns against duplicating his foolishness. The world's promises are hollow. The cycle leads down.

Personal, intimate knowledge of God's love and plan for our lives is our only protection. Without this, we too will be motivated by the cycle of wanting and striving.

## The Power To Change

The power of love to motivate and change is hardly news. Medical and behavior fields alike document love's strength. One person's love for another can bring about miracles. How much more can God's divine, pure, holy love transform us.

The apostle Paul experienced God's love and found it to control, urge, compel him in a life of faith. The world's value system could not hold him. He ministered from a pure heart.

Have you ever felt compelled, as Paul was, to do something? For me, writing this section of this book comes from that kind of urgency. This type of writing is new to me. I have felt timid and unsure of my ability. What's more, the opportunity came at a time when I was already carrying my quota of teaching, speaking and committee work. Two major projects, a speaking engagement and the final manuscript would all be due the same weekend. Yet I felt pulled toward the task of writing.

After talking about my concerns with my husband, I sat down for a long talk with McDougal, our dog. Mac ran loose before we moved here. Now we live in town. At first we took him to the lake shore to run. Then came the six-foot-leash law. So, to compensate, I began walking him three times a day. That's an hour and a half spent with the dog. Writing these chapters meant cutting Mac back to one significant walk a day.

Then, I needed a work space. I set up shop on a wobbly table in the basement. And every free minute, I headed downstairs. (Don't tell the trustees I've neglected the house.) A depressed lump of fur accompanied me. In the process, some things changed. Howard built a beautiful study desk with typing table for me.

Mac got over his depression. But still, every free minute it was down to the desk for me. And I loved it. I never grew tired of trying to get the words to come out right.

God-sent compulsions like this are fulfilling. Knowing God intimately makes us want to share Him through ministry—in my case, even in a new, intimidating ministry. An awareness of God's love motivated me.

A believer who lacks motivation to do God's work has lost sight of who God is and of how much He loves her. She needs to personally see and feel her importance to Him. If the church is a "quart down" in workers, it is probably also low in its corporate awareness of God's love. When God and His love are elevated, communicated, felt—people are motivated and committed to ministry. Love is action. A response is natural.

## What Can I Do?

Think back to when you first came to know the Lord. Wasn't part of that experience Paul's question: "Lord, what do you want me to do?" Realizing you were free from the negatives of sin and were loved by God combined to pull you into His work. "Lord, what can I do? Please, let me help!" You were compelled.

Wanting to pay back God is not the point. We are not capable of this. Rather, we need to be near the One who loves us and to be involved in what is important to Him. God didn't have to give us a place in winning back His fallen world. He could have used angels, created something new or simply accomplished it alone. He is capable. But He knew us. He knew that being loved creates a need to give. We need a position in His work, an avenue for expressing gratitude. Opportunity to minister is ours because of our need, not His.

## Increasing In Ability

Besides being motivated to minister, a second result of knowing God will be growth—an increased ability to minister effectively. One parsonage where we lived was built in a wooded area. Some 20 oak trees dotted our yard, almost shutting out the sun entirely. You can imagine the struggle we had trying to keep our yard from reverting back to a barren woods floor.

A neighbor, however, had cleared away trees near his house. I looked wistfully over the fence at his lush, thick grass and lovely flowers. My flowers grew tall and spindly; his were compact splashes of color. But what caught my attention was a row of pine trees he had planted beginning at the house and ending at the back of the lot by the river.

When we had moved into our house, the neighbor's trees near his house were already taller than our two-story home. The others decreased gradually in size until you could almost touch the top of the one at the back.

The trees all had been planted at the same time, had grown in the same soil and had had the same care. And yet, though at first the difference in them was hardly noticeable, eventually some trees towered 12-15 feet above others. The only variant had been their exposure to sunlight.

Just as sunlight had made a difference in those pines, so our exposure to God's love makes a difference in us. Larry Richards reminds us: "God is set on changing us. He didn't rescue us from our old way of life simply to let us settle back hopelessly into it. In His very first touch on your life, He had transformation in mind."[3]

But how much God is able to transform us depends on us. Variations in growth patterns are visible in any group of believers. Among the charter church members will be some who have grown tall and strong for the Lord. God's influence can be seen not only in their knowledge of Him, but in their lifestyle and attitudes.

Whether in worship, family life, or business, they live God's way. Others may consistently attend and support the church, yet show little of God's influence. Obviously, sitting on a church pew doesn't make for holiness. Your intimacy with God and with who He is makes the difference. Your relationship with God is the source of your growth.

The productive life is one in which God leads and redeemed men and women follow. It's an exciting adventure in partnership. Paul prayed that the Philippian believers would love God so completely that His purpose would be completed and perfected in them. This is God's goal for us.

## Daring To Be Involved

Few believers would say they do not want to be deeply involved with God. Few would admit not wanting to put forth the effort, to risk the outcome to minister for God. Even so, many of us live this way—afraid to look at who we are through the mirror of God's love and reluctant to accept our roles in God's plan. It is as if we believe that by not verbalizing our thoughts, God won't notice.

God notices. Silence has a voice all its own. He notices our absence and the unfilled places in His work.

Ray Ortlund regards our relationship with God as life's number one priority (see also the first section of this book): "...at whatever stage you are spiritually, commit your heart to the Person of God Himself in Jesus Christ."[4]

You may already be God's child. Even so, committing yourself to *intimately knowing* Him is the beginning of ministry.

Do you question who are you and why you are? Look in God's Word. See His plans for you.

Say *yes* to ministry.

## For Your Study

1. God's Word holds a promise of who you can be. Who does God want you to be? Relate your answer to William Barclay's statement that in God's knowledge of you is found a purpose, plan, design and task.

2. Describe an activity that requires discipline.
   What motivated you to complete the task?
   What were the rewards?

3. List the disciplines that will enable you to become the person God seeks as His minister.
   What will motivate you to grow toward this?
   What will be the rewards?

Footnotes:

1. Jonathan and David, Inc., Grand Rapids, Mich.
2. William Barclay, *The Letter to the Romans* (Philadelphia: The Westminster Press, 1957), p.120.
3. Larry Richards, *Born to Grow* (Wheaton, Ill.: Victor Books, 1982), p.42.
4. Raymond C. Ortlund, *Lord, Make My Life a Miracle* (Glendale, Calif.: Regal Books, 1976), p.2.

# 2
# *Yes, No,*
# *And*
# *How Many?*

A new Christian on her way to plan a meeting was asked by her non-Baptist mother, "Why do you have to have a meeting to plan your meeting?" Actually, a first meeting had been held to appoint a committee. Then the committee had had a meeting to decide what kind of meeting to have. Now the woman was attending a third meeting to plan "The Meeting." I'm glad her mother didn't know the whole story.

Some of us are so busy running to meetings that we can't accomplish anything real. Needs are present, but we're a long way from being responsible, God-led partners in meeting them. Our hearts are good, but we're spread so thin we're dangerous.

The world is filled with opportunities to make a statement in God's name, to be the one to make a difference. Involvement happens so naturally that we hardly notice. After all, God mentioned the *everwidening* circles of Judea, Samaria and out into the world. It's hard to know where to stop.

Yet, God expects us to be responsible in choosing how we

will minister. Exploding in all directions at once damages not only the object of our good intentions, but us too. Looking at God's Word, we realize that productive activities are planned and led by Him. And most often, it takes time to let God show us how a specific task is to be accomplished.

## Checking God's Plans

Think of David's attempt to move the ark of God to a permanent dwelling place (2 Sam. 6). The need was real. Yet because David didn't take time to check God's plan, a man died and the project had to be abandoned. David had put the ark on an ox cart. When the cart hit a rough spot and tipped, Uzzah reached out his hand to protect the ark from falling, and God killed him. Fear and confusion resulted. For three months, the ark was abandoned at the house of Obed-edom, the Gittite.

Meanwhile, David did some checking.

"God, why did you kill that man? We were doing a good thing for You."

"David, look in my law. You were in such a hurry you missed first base."

So, David became a student of the law. In his second attempt to move the ark, he followed God's plan and methods. The ox cart was replaced by the Sons of Kohath. After 30 feet, sacrifice was made. As a result of obedience, all Jerusalem celebrated. Trumpeting, shouting and leaping for joy signaled the ark's safe arrival in the temple. God led. His children obediently followed. Joy filled Israel.

And today the pattern remains unchanged. Before signing up, volunteering or starting a project, we need to stop and ask: 1) Do I see the need? 2) Am I the one called to meet this need? Only when both answers are yes is our ministry part of God's plan.

## Seeing The Need

John Stott tells us that Jesus' earthly tools for ministry were His eyes, His heart and His hands.[1] He used them in that order. He *looked* at people and *saw* their need. Determining what caused the need or who was to blame was not important. Looking and seeing was.

Watching, Jesus also felt what others were feeling. Empathy. It was as though He were in their positions. Then, having seen and felt the need, He reached to touch them with His hand. He did something about the need.

Ministry is intended to meet needs. Awareness and sensitivity are required. You may see a neighbor hurting, a problem at school, a person unemployed, a good idea floundering. Then God leads by personally showing *you* that something needs to be done.

Have you ever tried to get someone else to do what you felt needed doing? Perhaps your experience was like mine. A friend telephoned to ask me to give a devotional talk at a church shower. For some reason, I did not see the need for my involvement. What should I do? Do I say, "I'm sorry, I don't feel I should do it?" That doesn't sound very spiritual. But my feeling was real. My week was already too busy. Finally, I heard myself saying exactly that: "I'm sorry, I just don't feel I should do it."

"But..." I added quickly, "I won't leave you without anyone. Call back if you need me."

On the other end of the line was silence. Then I heard a weak, "Well, I'll pray about it." Strange response. Several days went by before I called her.

"Did you find someone to do the devotional talk?" I asked. Her reply surprised me.

"Oh, Roberta! I just knew all the time I was supposed to do it. But I was scared! I was hoping you would do it. But now that I'm working on it, I'm so excited!"

Both of us were capable of doing the devotional talk. But God had shown her the need, not me. So she had the plan, not I.

## Recognizing Your Assignments

On the other hand, have you ever encountered something you knew was yours to do? Often this happens to me when I'm asked to speak. First I check the calendar. Do I have time? Yes. Then I listen to what the inviter is saying. Do I see their need? Soon we're sharing ideas and feeling like old partners in ministry. It isn't at all unusual for me to jot down a Scripture portion. Sometimes I have a brief outline sketched out before we have said goodbye. God has shown me the need. I have no doubts.

But what happens when we say yes when we should say no? We may end up learning the hard way, as I did. One year I tried leading the social committee for our women's work. Church kitchens are not my thing. But I had been asked. Other than my feelings, I couldn't think of a single reason to say no.

The next few months were real sweat and strain. Finally, in despair I said to a friend, "I wish I were doing some of the secretarial things. I'm no good at this."

"Really?" she said, surprised by my honesty. "I like kitchen work. I'm not at all comfortable with my secretarial-type job."

With the committee's approval, we traded duties and lived happily the rest of the term. Both of us had said yes when we instinctively knew to say no.

Not trusting your feelings can do more than just get you into difficult jobs. You can end up taking on too many jobs. How do you explain the hyper-active, non-productive times caused by our over-commitment? Dare I address it in print? Let's ease into the answer:

God has a plan. We are part of that plan. He knows which part.

Scripture calls us an *alive* sacrifice for Him. Self-destruction and spiritual suicide can hardly be part of being alive.

Therefore, it is inconsistent to think that God, who wants us fully alive, would cause overbusyness. Burn-out is not His idea. He leads weary workers by still waters to revive them.

Conclusion: over-commitment, like all life's excesses, originates with the author of sin himself.

It's time to retire the bulging briefcase and the T-shirt decorated with Atlas holding up the world. Listening to God is the key. All opportunities that bear your name will come from Him. You will personally see the need.

## Being Called To Meet a Need

My decision not to do that shower devotional talk was based on more than a feeling. God expects us to think. And when I thought about what to do, I knew that although I was capable and had the resources, my problem was lack of time.

Our mental processes, Scripture, circumstances that bear God's signature and our feelings combine to indicate what God wants us to do. Following this, we wait for Him to open doors.

Waiting does not mean doing nothing. Some of God's leading is as clear as a handwritten invitation. Most often, He leads as we move toward doing what seems right. Call it "testing the wind" or "trying the doors," we take steps toward involvement and watch for God's leading.

When Abraham's servant found God's chosen bride for Isaac (Gen. 24), he said, "I being in the way of obedience and faith" was led to the right house. Reading the entire chapter you see the servant's detailed plan and how carefully he prayed for guidance. God led *as* he journeyed.

Sometimes, even though the need is clear to us, God doesn't give us the go-ahead signal. Early one year I was offered an exciting speaking opportunity. My calendar was clear. I had time to prepare. I wanted to say yes right away. However, when I discussed the invitation with my husband, he said, "No, I don't want you to go."

No? That hurt. Why was he doing this to me? Out of respect for him I turned down the offer, but I had a hard time accepting the closed door.

That fall Howard was hospitalized for a long, difficult stay. My days were spent by his bed doing as much as I could to make him comfortable. The nursing staff had been cut back. They hardly had time to take care of basics.

After a week of leaving Howard only long enough to check the mail, shower and change clothes, I was stopped by a nurse in the hospital hallway. "Roberta, I know how busy you are," she said. "I'm so thankful you have had time to sit with Howard." Suddenly I realized what day it was. Tears came to my eyes. If I had had my way, I would have been across the country ministering to a group of women. The person who really needed me would have been alone.

Now whenever I'm tempted to question a closed door, I recall my feelings that day. I hope you have felt God open and close a ministry for you. If so, you have a memory that can keep you from signing up for all good causes. You have experienced the long-term significance of God's leading. Holding out for God's "yes" or "no" means that the person selling those Atlas T-shirts will have lost the ability to con you into ineffective hyper-busyness.

## Focusing On Obedience

I like Philippians 1:12 and 13 according to Larry Richards: "Attack your difficulties with confidence and a due sense of responsibility, for God is at work in you, expressing His will in every situation as you keep your life in focus through obedience."[2]

We've just been looking at our responsibility in saying yes or no to ministry. But to effectively minister, we also need to look at personal qualities that fall under the heading of obedience.

In the next three chapters, we'll look at three I consider very important:

1. *Character*. God is looking for people who share His character in this world. People who act like Him.

2. *Competency*. God is looking for those who will pay the price to learn necessary skills for ministry.

3. *Attitude*. God is looking for a positiveness in His ministers—positiveness toward Him and His plan.

## For Your Study

1. Circle the words that apply to you:

    non-involved      over-involved      balanced

    leader      joiner      apathetic

2. Rate yourself on the following on a scale of 1-10 (1, always no; 10, always yes)
   *I tend to say yes to everything.
   *I allow time for the unexpected.
   *I feel guilty about saying no.
   *I can balance home, church and outside involvement.
   *I seek God's opinion before making time commitments.
   *I know how to seek God's opinion.

## Footnotes

1. John R.W. Stott, *Who Is My Neighbor?* (London: Inter-Varsity Press, 1975), pp.6-9.
2. Richards, p.134.

# 3
# A
# *Family*
# *Resemblance*

One summer I was camp pastor for junior girls at a camp in Minnesota. My husband Howard was teaching on staff, and Mike and Dave, our junior-age boys, had accompanied us and were having the time of their lives.

As I walked to the chapel for the service one warm evening, some excited little girls joined me. We played together on the way and after hugging goodbye, I knew I needed to comb my hair to be presentable. But I had no mirror. Then I remembered having seen a picture just inside the study door. I could look at my reflection in the glass.

The picture was hung so that when I looked into it, I was eye-level with the artist's conception of our Lord. For one brief space in time, I stood looking at my image reflected in the face of Jesus. I thought of our Conference women's theme that year: "Like You, Lord."

The reflection was so clear that you could not know which was the portrait. I don't remember combing my hair. I do remember tears coming to my eyes as I knelt to pray. I feel tears now as I think of it. My Lord and I as one.

## His Mark On Your Life

It is one thing to believe that God is real. It is quite another to seek to look like Him in habit and lifestyle here on earth. Yet, this is what He asks of us—to have God-like character.

One definition of the word "character" is: "A sign or token placed upon an object as an indication of some special fact, as ownership or origin."[1] Years ago in England the word "character" referred to an instrument used for marking. Later the word came to include the mark made by the instrument. If a statesman sent a letter, he would use an instrument to make an impression of his private seal on the envelope. The impression indicated the letter's origin, authenticity and ownership. It was the statesman's "character."

Another definition of the word "character" is: "The aggregate of distinctive qualities belonging to an individual, or race; the stamp of individuality impressed by nature, education or habit."[2]

This addresses the qualities that make up the individuality of a person or group of persons. For example, families, nationalities, political parties and special interest groups are recognized by common traits or qualities.

To this day, if my mother were to walk down the street of Morehead, Ky., someone would stop her and ask, "Oh, now which of the McBrayers girls are you?" Several families of the McBrayer clan have lived in the area. Even cousins bear a physical resemblance. And if you were to spend time with them, you would detect other family characteristics such as work ethic, value system, belief in God.

Character, then, reflects our deepest nature. When our nation began, great emphasis was placed on developing Godlike character. Honesty, dedication and commitment were taught in the home. Schools also presented these as ideals. Pastors and politicians alike preached their value, using such synonyms as "goodness," "worthwhileness," "successfulness."

## A Key To Success

The success of great men and women was said to be determined by their character. A book about famous men published in 1922 stated: "Certain outstanding characteristics in the boyhoods of these men were responsible in a great part for their later success. Such characteristics are worthy of emulation by the boys and girls of today."[3]

Some of the great men listed were:

Thomas A. Edison, the boy who always finished whatever he started.

Theodore Roosevelt, the boy who developed his body as well as his mind.

George Washington Goethals, the boy who shaped his own career.

John Wanamaker, the boy who built with his brains instead of with bricks.

Herbert Hoover, the boy who would not let other people make up his mind.

John J. Pershing, whose perseverance fitted him for his great opportunity.

Calvin Coolidge, who was ready for his great opportunity when it came to him.[4]

Because these American heroes had character, they offered hope during years of war and depression.

Character development was taken seriously in the past. Homes and classrooms continued to teach Godly character until the 1960s. Then, a change began. Values were looked down on. Honesty was said to be poor business. People were advised to "look out for number 1." Survive. Do whatever it takes to keep surviving.

Now, after 25 years, part of our nation seems to be turning back to our early-day values. Recently 27 prominent educators and citizens urged American schools to take action to counter the serious decline in character among youth. The mix of liberals and conservatives who made the plea were concerned about teenage suicides and homicides and the rise of out-of-wedlock births.

They pointed to a general weakening of institutions—such as family, church, community and schools—that once built character in the young.[5]

## The Meaning Of Character

Yet I wonder, if we come again to a place where Godlike character is held up as the ideal, are we believers prepared to model this way of living? Do our children understand what Godlike character means? Or has the world had such an impact on us that very little of God can be seen in us?

Think of Paul's prayer for the Philippian believers. He wanted them to love God so much that they would pursue "the highest and the best...distinguishing the moral differences." Excellence in decisions, choices and morality was to set them apart from the world in which they lived.

God waits to implant his character in our lives—His multi-faceted character as described in Galatians 5:22—love, joy, peace, patience, kindness, goodness, faithfulness, gentleness, self-control. Accepting Him means that the tiny seed of who He is is placed within us. For a period of time very little evidence of God may be visible. A new way of life slowly begins to show, but nothing you could call a piece of fruit, or a flower in bloom. Nothing mature.

Like growing marigolds, the life of the flower is in the seed when it is planted. The first changes occur hidden from sight, underground. You water and feed something you can't see, but by faith you believe it is alive and growing.

Then a tiny piece of green peeks through the soil. Leaves begin to form. Time passes. The stem grows strong, more leaves appear. Finally, a bud. You water more and feed. More time passes. One day you walk in your garden and there it is! The flower that was in the seed is visible. What a delight! Having seen the flower, you're hooked on growing marigolds forever.

## A Gradual Transformation

So it is with God's character within you. Gradually, a little love breaks through. Then some self-control. A little peace begins to show. Each facet of character is strengthened in you. Your nature and life habits are influenced.

The good news is that as you continue to walk with God, all of His character can be fully displayed in you at once. Think of the beauty of it. Of the possibility.

Elderly apostle John wrote: "...that we may have boldness in the day of judgment, because as He is, so are we in this world" (1 Jn. 4:17, KJV). We can stand in judgment knowing we have looked like God while living on earth. Now, that's a miracle!

Look at the list of God's characteristics again. Do the words overwhelm you? Some are big, difficult to grasp. But the concepts are so important. Think of the difference they could make in you and your ministry.

There is little need to look further than a local church to see the results of their absence. Maybe the lack is more visible because God's people gather to plan and to do God's work here. Godlike lifestyle and actions are expected. Their absence glares

and shocks. The same absence in the work place tends to be ig-
nored among the worst, but commonplace, world's standards.

How do you feel when you see sloppiness, apathy or dishonesty
in God's church. Things are planned that never get started. Needs
gather dust in committees. Projects are abandoned halfway
through. Believers give in to temptation and see little need to
confess.

## Not A Debatable Choice

The Scriptural call to be like God is not a debatable choice.
Excellence is not optional for God's people. Mediocrity or sin-
fulness are unthinkable.

"But, I'm not perfect!" you protest.

God knows this. Refusing to try is the sin.

Our older son captured this concept in one of his grade school
compositions. He was writing about one of his "bad" days—
which at his age were not infrequent. In the paper he listed all
the messes he had been in that day, most of them his own fault.
The list was enough to discourage a less hearty soul and make
him want to stay in bed for a week. Not Mike.

He concluded his paper by saying,, "But one bad day doesn't
make an all bad boy." Mike wasn't afraid to try again. I wanted
to cheer.

Other lists of character possibilities are given in Scripture.
One precedes the passage about the Fruit of the Spirit. They are
the characteristics of those who do not walk close to God:

"What human nature does is quite plain. It shows itself in
immoral, filthy, and indecent actions; in worship of idols and
witchcraft. People become enemies, they fight, become jealous,
angry, and ambitious. They separate into parties and groups; they
are envious, get drunk, have orgies and do other things like these
(Gal. 5:19, TEV).

How I wish we were exempt and protected from these. But we are not. Failures will come. At times we will need to ask forgiveness and accept that "one bad day doesn't make an all bad person."

But one truth stands for all time: the development of God's character within you is more than an attainable goal. It is a promised possibility that affects your ministry.

Are you developing God's character within?

The answer is important.

## For Your Study

1. Agree/disagree: There has been a lessening of emphasis on character development in society and in the church during the past few decades. What leads you to this belief?

2. Agree/disagree: Christian character is based on the development of Spirit Fruit as described in Galatians 5:22.

3. Which of these distinctive qualities of God's family are evidenced in your life?

Which is the most fully developed? Why?

Which are underdeveloped? How can their growth be encouraged?

4. How have you tried to teach these traits to those you influence? Include who you influence and by what means.

5. Pray for yourself, your church and those you influence.

## Footnotes:

1. Webster, s.v. character.
2. Ibid.
3. Carroll Everett and Charles Francis Reed, *When They Were Boys* (Dansville, N.Y.: F.A. Owen Publishing Co., 1922), preface.
4. Ibid, Table of Contents.
5. "Schools Get 'F' in Character Building," *U.S. News & World Report*, Dec. 3, 1984, p. 10.

# 4
## *Fit, Proper and Qualified*

Have you ever heard someone say, "Oh, I'd give anything if I could..."? Maybe you've said it. A friend completed a complicated piece of handwork, or ran a marathon or memorized your favorite book of Scripture.

What they did isn't nearly as important as the fact that you just declared you'd do anything to be able to accomplish the same. Really? Anything? Does that include spending time to learn the skill and then disciplining yourself to complete the project?

Oh!

Somewhere lying dormant in the back of our minds is at least a bushel of "I wish I hads" Summer projects that become fall projects that become—well, you know. Sometimes these wishes are not just in our minds. How about the trunk full of quilt pieces, all those walnut boards, the new running shoes still in the box, the exercise bike in the basement? We want to do so many things, but not badly enough to prepare ourselves to do them. The tragedy is that what is true in our everyday lives is also true in the area of the Lord's work that is our ministry.

God has given you a gift(s) to be used in His work. You know about 1 Corinthians 12:11: "All these (achievements and abilities) are inspired and brought to pass by one and the same (Holy) Spirit, who apportions to each person individually (exactly) as He chooses." Your gifts are meant to be opened, examined and used.

## Unwrapping Your Gift

Think about Christmas. Perhaps you wanted a band saw and there it was. You knew the minute you picked up the package. You ripped off the wrapping and checked the instructions—er, kinda. From that point on, the only evidence that you were still in the house was the sawdust circulated through the furnace pipes and tracked up the basement stairs.

Before long, your house showed evidence that someone had the skills and equipment to remodel and build. By now, your saw has a well-loved look and some new attachments.

For you it wasn't—isn't—a burden to use the saw. You wanted and needed it. The saw is great!

Now think of God's work. Our world needs Godly reconstruction, and the Holy Spirit has given you a gift, a tool, to help do that. Then why aren't you busy? Don't you want His gift? Don't you want to be part of His plans?

Does this sound harsh? Maybe our reluctance isn't that we don't want to be part of God's work. Perhaps you've opened your gift but can't figure out what it is or how to use it.

Some gifts are like that. You can hold them upside down and shake them, and still you can't figure out what they are. You talk to people and read the right books, but your gift is still a mystery. That's okay. Don't worry. Don't be frustrated. Give yourself time. Meanwhile, do something helpful and fun.

Everyone can help. Everyone enjoys helping. Relax. Look around you at what needs to be done in your church. Now, what part would you *like* to do? Fold bulletins? Do Sunday school follow-up? Help in the kitchen? Smile in the foyer? Take a turn in the nursery? Deliver some cookies? Someone has to do these things. People who do them are the burden-lifters of the church.

As a bonus, somewhere along the way while being helpful, you may identify your special gift. It is possible to find your place while enjoying being helpful. For example, you find out you are one of those "super smilers." People really respond to your warm greeting. You like doing it. Sure enough, next election you're on the ballot as greeter or usher.

## With Or Without Labels

Or you may discover that you are the only one in church who can calm that child who cries for Mom halfway through every service. That's a good feeling—the only one. So you join that ministry permanently. The fact is that it is possible to minister without identifying your gift. Isn't that a relief! You don't have to search for a label before going to work. You can enjoy doing, and trust the labels to God.

Now, having found a place of ministry, labeled or not, you'll soon discover a lot you don't know. Few of us are like Peter, whose first sermon had an impact on a whole city. Most of us grow into our ministries. We tend to start at the bottom with a little exposure, a small success, and work our way into increasing responsibility. All the while, we learn, try, pray and enjoy. God-given gifts are a kind of do-it-yourself project with God's presence as the power pack.

Isn't it interesting that just as God gives us His character, the Fruit of the Spirit, in seedling form, so He also gives us His gifting. It is possible to be called and given a vision long before we are capable of handling it.

When God called my husband Howard to be a pastor, he was in his 30s. He was a good businessman and church worker. But a pastor? Some people didn't see much possibility. One of his best friends seriously questioned him. A pastor? Really? Yes. Howard knew that he was called. There wasn't a doubt in his mind. And he was just as sure that he wasn't ready for his first church.

God led him through seminary training, and from youth pastor, to interim pastor, before opening the door for his first church. Amazing. The first Sunday Howard stood in his own pulpit, he was fully equipped. He had paid his dues for doing what he had known for three years God wanted him to do.

People whose ministry does not require formal education or other preparation also grow into and with their responsibilities. They find that being faithful to the task opens the door for deepening levels of involvement and widening areas of service.

In a beginning speech class in my second year of college, the professor said, "Your final exam will be a three-act play with five characters. You will perform this in a 36-inch-square area without costumes or props." Talk about acute trauma! When the groans subsided, she added, "Now, your first assignment will be to stand in front of the class and read the four-line poem I'm distributing."

Can you believe that when it came time to do our plays, we had no more stress than it took to read our first poem? The teacher had guided and developed our ability for a whole year. She had taken us through a series of increasingly more difficult assignments, until we were ready to do what she had planned.

God is like this. He has an area in which He wants you to work. And He guides you into being fully competent for that work.

A *Christian Leadership Newsletter* defines competency as:

1. Having requisite ability or qualities; FIT
2. Rightfully belonging: PROPER
3. Legally qualified or capable; ABLE, SUFFICIENT[1]

Fit, Proper, Qualified, Sufficient. In each of these areas God has a part and you have a part. Remember, you and God are partners. Becoming competent is a two-step project.

## Basic Competency

Our basic competency is the initial skill development that trains us for the work we feel God wants us to do. For a church chairman, it may be a working knowledge of administrative skills. For the head of the social committee, basic competency may be organization plus understanding food service techniques.

There is always a temptation to skip the basic competencies. After all, if God has called you, He will show you how. Some people go so far as to feel that the proof of their being in an area of God's calling is that they have not been trained for the responsibility. They seem to think some kind of mystical enabling cloak has been dropped on them, that training isn't necessary.

I can handle things quite well in my kitchen. The number of people to prepare for doesn't matter. However, the church kitchen is something else. I can just see me without training trying to orchestrate a sit-down dinner for 200. I'd be on my knees in the pantry before the salad course, if I lasted that long. Cooking for crowds takes a special knowledge base. A lot of God-given ability is needed also, as well as hands-on training.

God has given you a brain. Remember? You are expected to learn what you need to learn. He may lead you to the right place to learn, but He rarely does for you what He has equipped you to do for yourself.

God likes things done beautifully, in order, with joy and peace. He knows the good feeling you have in doing something well that can be given back to Him as a love offering. He understands your need to contribute. That's why He allows you to be responsible for such a large part, not just in ministry, but also in preparing for ministry.

## The Need To Help

Parents of small children can see first-hand the human need to contribute, to be helpful. One day when I was vacuuming our home, one of our small boys was crawling along behind me. Every once in awhile he would unplug the sweeper, look at me and grin, and then plug it back in. The interruption was cute at first, then it began to annoy me. I was ready to yell, "Don't touch that plug!" in typical mother volume when I wondered if he thought he was helping.

Small as he was, he knew I couldn't work without the sweeper plugged in. Sure enough, on other cleaning occasions when I let him help get out the sweeper, unwind the cord, and plug it in— he was happy. It was as though he had gotten Mom organized and into her day. He'd play until he heard the sweeper stop, then run to help rewind the cord and put the machine away.

Adults are no different. We have a natural desire to make a valid contribution. In God's work, helping is a natural by-product of our love and His. "God, let me help. Please let me help."

But because we're adults, there's no need to annoy God or slow down progress. We must take time to discover where we're needed and then be guided into learning the necessary skills. Sometimes this process requires several years of our lives. Whatever amount of time is needed, in the end we are able to function in a productive way.

A sign in a deli near our home says, "Every job is a self-portrait of the person who did it. Autograph your work with excellence." This is a good goal. Let's prepare ourselves for ministering with a touch of excellence.

Not that we want to get hung up on perfection. We don't want to spend our lives stuck in one spot polishing and repolishing the same piece of work to make it better. We want excellence that allows us to efficiently perform our assignments and move on to the next God-sent adventure. This kind of excellence comes from being prepared to serve.

## Specific Competency

Specific competency has to do with preparing for a specific opportunity within our ministry. Some people seem to enjoy the basic preparation. We all have encountered the career student. She is forever learning but is never able to leave the Halls of Ivy to do anything with what she's learned. Such people have felt God's call and have launched zealously into preparation and then stopped there.

Perhaps the reason is that they've organized all their skills, and don't want to mess them up. They are like the homemaker who cleans house and makes everyone sit around doing nothing. The homemaker didn't clean the house so it could be lived in. She cleaned it so it would be clean. Our reason for learning skills makes all the difference in the world.

For others, fear is involved. It is scary to present yourself as capable of making a contribution in some corner of God's world. Murphy's Law is always there to contend with. If something embarrassing can happen, it will.

Years ago I was invited to speak at a girls club rally. I knew God could use me in front of people. I had confidence in His leading. I prepared myself as well as I could. In fact, I practiced my presentation so much that my boys could almost do it with me word for word. I had planned to make a huge sandwich with all the condiments, illustrating God's gifting filled with components of love and spread with His promises.

The evening arrived. I had my picnic basket loaded with notes, tablecloth, sandwich-makings, etc. Things went well. Why not? God had led and I had prepared. That's a good working partnership. Well, I should say things went well until time for the mustard. It represented one of God's promises that added flavor to our gifting.

Suddenly the mustard dispenser had a nervous reaction to the crowd. (It's the only logical explanation.) The next thing I knew, instead of landing on the bread the mustard dispensed itself on the carpeting right in front of the pulpit.

"Oh, no!" I said under my breath.

As soon as the service was over, we rushed to work on the mustard blob. They assured me that it would come out of the carpeting. But we all know how stubborn mustard can be.

Thinking about it on the way home, I just knew what I had tried to teach would be forever upstaged by the mustard. In fact, were it not for encouraging friends, I'm not sure I would have tried a creative approach to teaching Scripture again for a long time.

This type of thing, and worse, happens to everyone who gets involved on any level of ministry. If enough things go wrong in a row without God sending someone to pat us on the back to say, "That's okay. Keep going"—we tend to give up and go back to sitting on the last pew. One embarrassing event is enough to cause us to allow our fear of the unknown, of the unplanned for, to defeat us. Perhaps our problem is our damaged egos. Nevertheless, the problem is real. We're afraid.

## Overcoming Fear

God tells us that regardless of what the fear might be, it has not been sent by Him. He says He gives us a spirit of "power and of love and of a calm and well-balanced mind and discipline and self-control'' (2 Tim. 1:7b). Wow!

Notice again the emphasis on the use of our minds. We need to think before giving in to any fear. After all, our spirit of uncertainty is only good for creating another round of parties in the enemy's camp. They celebrate when a believer cancels her contribution to God's work. I don't like this.

## Handling Our Deepest Hurts

Past hurts have the same negative influence over us that fear does. Sadly, we have to face the fact that our deepest hurts come from within God's church, not from the world. It's a cruel trick.

Christ's teaching made it clear that the believers' ability to love, nurture and encourage each other was to be the primary witness to the world that He is God. Is it any wonder that this has become the main arena of our fight with evil? Is it any wonder that our first tendency is to lash out against each other, instead of joining forces against Satan, who set us up?

The old grade-school tactic was to get your two worst enemies fighting each other so they'd forget about you. You'd be free to go about doing whatever you wanted. As long as believers can be tricked into bickering with each other, the enemy is loose to do as he pleases.

It isn't possible to control the other believer, her feelings and actions. What is possible is to take control of your life. Ask God to come close to the believer who has come against you. Ask God to help them through whatever is causing their need to make hurtful statements or behave as they do. Do what you can to restore peace. Admit your part in the problem.

But all the while, regardless of what happens, keep your eyes and energy directed toward following God, doing what He wants you to do. The centrality of God in your life can become a positive force in an enemy's life.

Fears and hurts are devices that can keep you from beginning and continuing the ministry you've been called and prepared to do. Non-involvement makes you as ineffective as the person who could care less about God's plan. Either way nothing is being done. Don't let anything hold you back from using the gift God has given in the area He has opened.

Earning certificates or striving for greater ones is not the goal. Spending time making sure you are loved also is not the goal. The goal is to become proficient in your area and then to minister. Step out. Accept the opportunities God gives.

## Look Out For The Trap

There's another trap that you can easily fall into on your way to being competent in a specific opportunity. Perhaps you've encountered the individual who is well trained and has been assigned, or elected to a responsibility. But she never does it. She may attend all the important meetings, shuffle the right amount of paperwork, pray proper prayers. She may have a committee that meets regularly. But when you look for evidence that something is happening in her area, it's not there.

This type of individual has gone one step beyond the person who never stops training herself. She passed up the person who started but quit. She's accepted a responsibility and continues to hold the position. But where preparation is the ultimate for the perennial trainee and approval for the fearful one, holding office seems to be the goal for her. Her vision stops with being elected.

Often such an individual is a long-standing member of the local church. She is an effective communicator. She is well respected. Even so, she isn't doing anything.

Personality, prominence, attractiveness, natural ability are positives. But she uses these positives to attain a position in the church, not to function.

She is a good person. She doesn't intend to stop part of God's work. But she is fooling herself into thinking that her presence is better than the best efforts of someone younger, less experienced, untried, etc. Holding office seems to be her reward for longevity and a good name. She would be among the first to be shocked by the truth that nothing is being done.

She has fallen into the trap of believing that she is fulfilling an important responsibility in ministry when all the time she is totally unproductive.

Nowhere in Scripture is there a more beautiful picture of a productive worker than in Psalm 1. Here we see a person who has turned his back on the world's ways. In fact, he refuses to be anywhere near something that might tempt him to go back on his covenant agreement to love and follow Holy God. He refuses to walk, stand or sit in a place of temptation.

He has allowed God to plant him where God wants him to be. He hasn't brought any hidden agendas to his ministry and his place of serving.

## God Can Be Trusted

God cares about your contribution to His work. He is to be trusted to put you into the place that is most productive. Your part is to have said a firm no to the world, to submit to His planting, and then to put your roots deep into the nourishment He provides. Fruitfulness is the promised by-product of meeting these conditions.

It seems impossible that any child of God would choose to name his place of usefulness, to do his own thing. Those who do have lost sight of why God gifted and called them. It is His work.

Ephesians 4:12 tells us: ''His intention was the perfecting and the full equipping of the saints (His consecrated people) (that they should do) the work of ministering toward building up Christ's body (the church)." Our gifting is intended to build up and equip each other so that together we can be used to build God's church on earth. It is a high, together calling.

In 1 Corinthians 14:12 we are told to be "eager and ambitious to possess spiritual endowments and manifestations of the (Holy) Spirit, (concentrate on) striving to excel and to abound (in them) in ways that will build up the church." This is why we seek to be fully competent and to use our competency in God's work. This is why we seek to excel. And we are not alone in our calling.

"Let everything be constructive and edifying and for the good of all" (1 Cor. 14:26 b). God's work is done by all for the good of all. The plural *you* of the New Testament speaks of the necessity of doing the work together. Each of us is be prepared to function in harmony with all the others.

There are no greater or lesser responsibilities in God's sight. His organizational chart is a circle with Himself at the center. All ministries lie within equal distance of His approval, guidance and power. All require our best.

Time for some questions. Have you found a place to serve? If so, have you done your part in equipping yourself to do the work well? Are you seeking excellence in the performance of your responsibilities?

The questions may not be easy to answer.

Ask God to help.

## For Your Study

1. Agree/disagree: It is not necessary to be able to name your spiritual gift before going to work for the Lord.

2. Describe how God has increased your ability to minister.

3. How would you help someone confirm which of their gift(s) to use? How would you help them begin to minister?

4. What is your greatest need:
      *to find a place to serve
      *to equip yourself with better skills
      *to use the knowledge you now have
      *to say no to some fear
      *to function in your assigned area
      *to strive for excellence
      *to be more like the tree in Psalm 1

Footnotes:

1. *Christian Leadership Letter*, (Monrovia, Calif.: World Vision International, Aug. 1981), p.3.

# 5
## Sunshine
## Or Rain,
## My Choice

This day I woke up knowing it was time to clean house. The night before, I had left the shades up, hoping for sunshine to wake me in the morning. But as I opened my eyes, I saw dull gray. I felt as gloomy as the weather. I grabbed for my nondescript bulk of chenille that serves as my housecoat and which fit my mood perfectly. Breakfast for the family was haphazard. What a way to start a day!

Living in a parsonage usually requires a neat outfit and makeup early in the morning. Not this day! A pair of the boys' old jeans suited me fine. A baggy sweatshirt blotched with paint and a pair of unmatching socks rounded out my outfit. Never mind makeup. I had work to do.

Usually cleaning house is fun. Everything takes on a fresh glow. Around noon you start a pot of hearty stew. By supper the orderly house is filled with good smells. Not this day. I struggled all forenoon rearranging messes and creating new ones. Finally, I gave up and went outside. Supper would have to come out of those strange containers in the fridge. What was wrong with me?

Chuck Swindoll says that the single most important decision you make everyday of your life is your choice of attitude.[1]

Ah.

I had *chosen* to be depressed even before I had gotten out of bed. I even dressed the part. And worse yet, everything and everyone in my world paid the price.

The word "attitude" means "posture, position or mood." The Latin word from which it is derived means "suited."[2] In the case of a ship, its attitude indicates its position in relationship to the water. When the attitude is level, the ship is suited to its purpose. Listing (tilting) or tipping—improper attitudes—reduce the ship's suitability. People and property are endangered when this happens. Sinking, of course, is entirely the wrong attitude.

The youth group of the first church my husband pastored prided themselves on their annual early spring canoe trip. Being new to Minnesota, we didn't know much about canoes. However, this didn't keep Howard from going along and taking our boys. During the outing, he and our son Dave decided to navigate together. Sure enough, halfway down the river they hit a rock, and the canoe tipped over. The exact cause remains their secret. However, they got a good feel for how cold a Minnesota river can be in early spring.

As long as their canoe's attitude was positive, the trip was great. The scenery was beautiful. Navigating was a new, exhilarating challenge. When the canoe tipped, the fun ended.

## It's Our Choice

A canoe is an inanimate, unthinking object. External forces or lack of guidance cause its change in attitude. People, however, have the ability to think and choose. In one sense, we can decide what attitudes will dominate our lives. A lack of sunshine hadn't forced me to be negative on my cleaning day. Grumbling and slouching through the day had been my idea.

Yet, like the canoe, my attitude also was determined by my relationship to something other than myself. As believers, our attitudes are measured by how we are in relationship to God. When our minds and spirits are in tune with Him, we are suited for productive living. Negativism comes when we allow elements of our environment to influence us. God's presence can create a mood of sunshine where there is none. Whether or not it does is up to us.

Jim Rohn of Adventure in Achievement warns about five diseases of attitude:

*Indifference*: the mild approach to life

*Indecision*: a thief of opportunity

*Doubt*: one of the worst being self-doubt

*Worry*: the real killer. In its final states it reduces you to begging.

*Overcaution*: Some people will never have much. They're too cautious.[3]

Looks like a list of old companions. At one time or another I've struggled with them all. Sometimes I've won, sometimes I've lost.

Indifference to God was the problem on my sunless day. Operating on overload, I had skipped my time with Him in favor of tackling the job. The energy and impetus that comes from being with His Word was not there. His statement on what was and wasn't important was not available to me. Ministry to my family was out of the question. All my energy went into being depressed.

## A Constant Temptation

Tiredness and busyness often lie at the bottom of negative moods. In today's pace these are hard to avoid. Even so, we choose their influence and length of rule. The temptation is always there. But we have no excuse for allowing it to use us as a permanent address. God's presence is to fill our lives and influence our living.

Just as a small hatch carelessly left open will allow a ship to take on water, so the world's value system can slosh into your life through tiny, hardly noticeable openings. At first you don't realize what is happening. Then a storm comes, a crisis occurs, a conflict or temptation appears, and you begin to list. You tell yourself that you don't need time with God. You know how to clean house and don't need His instruction. Yet skill is not the problem. Priorities and mood are. Becoming negative can happen so easily.

Negativism is an attitude disease that can grip groups, as well as individuals. It starts with a few people complaining about a new program or method or demands on their time. Their complaint may be legitimate, but their intent is not to correct the problem. They're just grumbling. It's infectious. Stand near them long enough and you'll grumble too. An amazing spirit of comradeship comes from being discontented together. The time comes when en masse you defy anyone to try to turn you positive.

Negativism is natural to sinful beings. That's us. Psalm 1 gives the progression. We lean toward some bad counsel, stand around to talk about it, and find we think and live by the negative influence.

Sin must be made palatable, thus—enter duplicity. Wrong must be made to look right if we are to live with it. Cynicism and criticism wear the masks of discernment and concern. Slander becomes burden-sharing. The way out of the negative pattern is difficult.

Because my husband is an excellent golfer, people ask for help with their persistent problems. A new way to grip the club or to position themselves over the ball may be needed. They listen and try the new approach. Once. Twice. Maybe a couple of rounds. Then, the self-defeating hook or slice is back. Holding the club differently was too hard. The new stance didn't feel natural. Living with the problem is preferred to change. Says Howard, "Few people will spend the time needed to correct a poor golfing habit."

Changing our attitude is even more difficult. To admit the need to change is to be willing to face new thought patterns, communication and behavior. Like water eroding a hillside, negative patterns wear deeply into our lives. Yet, if we are to minister effectively, we must change.

Cleaning house is more than removing clutter and dirt. You are ministering to all who live in your house by freshening and organizing tools and comforts of living. Early in the afternoon of that gray, depressing day, God managed to get through to me. By six p.m. the house was fresh and inviting. Supper was more than leftovers. Thankfully, my attitude had been a one-time event. Changing wasn't difficult. Worship and self-discipline did the trick. My problem had been in the gloomy way I had started the day.

## Vulnerable At Every Stage

As I've said, ministry involves beginning and continuing. And attitude diseases can attack us during both stages. Negativism can keep us from ever beginning to minister. Or other attitude problems may plague us as we learn to minister and are involved in carrying out our commitment.

On the matter of getting started, whenever I'm reluctant to attempt some ministry, I recall my Dad's advice: "Do something, even if it's wrong." The thought of mustering all my courage and charging off toward potential disaster makes me laugh. But it does something else too. I'm reminded that you can't predict the outcome of anything. So get going.

Our last year's church chairman put it another way as he urged us to start implementing our planning document: "God can't steer a parked car," he told us.

You have to be moving in some direction before God can steer you His way. Haven't you noticed that a surge of energy and excitement usually accompanies your decision to move out—to try something? You can't wait to tell everybody.

"I'm going to be teaching sixth grade boys this fall."

"I've decided to help with the church welcome wagon."

"They've asked me to help follow-up newcomers."

Most of the time we're in a cold sweat. We know we aren't quite ready. But it feels so good to be holding a God-given responsibility. Everyone should know that saying yes to Holy God is great. Don't let an attitude disease rob you of this joy.

My first elected church position was White Cross chairman of our women's missionary service. I bought a new notebook, sharpened my pencil and went to the first officers meeting. I was so proud. I was an officer. The job wasn't much. Once a year I mailed in a check and mentioned the ministry in a program. So I mailed and mentioned. It was great.

Never mind that it was a small job. God had called me to it. That made it the most important assignment on earth. Maybe it took only seven minutes to do my part. But the brief time was spent doing exactly what I knew God wanted me to do. Thank You, God, that a disease of attitude didn't rob me of the joy.

## Wearing Well

But what about long-term ministry? The feeling of privilege in a new job may float you through for awhile. But how about six months later, six years later, 60 years? Will your attitude stay healthy?

Long before the age of discipling, I knew women who were going by the textbook. I have such warm memories of being taught how to serve and shown what I could do. My Sunday school service began with one woman saying she enjoyed hearing me read Scripture at women's missionary service. Would I read to her primaries a story she had selected? Later, she said, "Do you have a story you would like to read?" Then, "Let me show you how to do a flannelgraph. I think you would enjoy this."

The day came when she turned the department over to me. She wasn't retiring. She was moving to another position. Her last words were, "I'm just around the corner in the beginner department if you need me." She was and I did.

In the next few years, she walked me through staffing, training teachers and replacing myself so I could move to an empty slot. A few years ago I was guest speaker in that church. Guess who helped organize the day? Still working. So positive in her relationship with God that she will never stop serving. She was suited to life-long ministry because of her relationship with Him.

"But I've delivered 785 casseroles, chaperoned 65 bus trips, logged 200 hours in the nursery and attended more than 2 million committee meetings. I've had it!" you may be protesting.

How precious are positive thinkers who never retire from serving the Lord. Their tasks change. God's assignments for them vary in importance. Still, they live every day working for Him. Faithful through all of life's changing circumstances, no disease of attitude has kept them from the joy of ministry.

## Half-Baked Potatoes

Positiveness is found in many Bible personalities. My favorite is Paul. He's amazing! In Philippians 1, he writes from prison. Hardly a place for positive productivity. Even without prison he should have been sick and tired of all the side roads his ministry kept taking. He constantly faced being detained, wounded or defamed. Worse yet, brothers and sisters in the Lord inflicted discouragements.

He is writing from a prison in Rome. Preaching Christ in this city had been his life-long dream—but from a cell? Sounds more like a nightmare. Listen to his feelings:

"Now I want you to know and continue to rest assured, brethren, that what (has happened) to me (this imprisonment,) has actually only served to advance and give a renewed impetus to the (spreading of the ) good news —of the Gospel" (Phil. 1:12).

He has not said one word about his visit to Rome not living up to his expectations. If you had served him a half-baked potato in a restaurant, he would have replied politely, "Thank you. I've never tried baked potatoes like this." Paul chose not to see things from a negative slant. "So this is where you can use me, Lord. What shall we do today?"

An unfilled preaching task existed because of Paul's imprisonment. Boldness and fresh confidence led some people to try to fill the need. Others saw an opportunity to take center stage with their preaching skills. Note Paul's response:

"But what does it matter, so long as either way, whether in pretense (for personal ends) or all honesty (for the furtherance of the Truth), Christ is being proclaimed? (Phil 1:18).

Paul's worst enemy could stand in his former pulpit. As long as God's Word was preached, Paul was content. See why he amazes me? The personal possessive tense is missing from his spiritual vocabulary. "My" is usually a very important word. My job, my territory, my place. How could Paul be so unselfish, so positive?

His formula for positiveness is included in the Philippian letter. Our thought patterns are the key. We are to think about things that are true, worthwhile, just, pure and gracious (Phil 4:8,9). In other words, a given circumstance plus correct thinking equals positiveness.

Serving God was the central theme of Paul's life. Confinement, cruelty and frustrated goals were good for five minutes of after-dinner talk, but that was all. It's like having your high school football team win the state championship and listening to your injured quarterback tell about it. He recounts every detail of the game without a single mention of his playing injured.

Everyone around him knows he was injured. They're X-raying, bandaging, giving instructions, patting his hand (that's his Mom). But the quarterback's mind is on the game. He feels pain, but it is not the focus of his life.

One day on my way to shop I met a modern-day saint waiting on a cold streetcorner for a bus. In her 80s, she'd been to church to do a "couple hours' work" for the Sunday school. Did the conversation focus on the cold weather or the inconvenience of waiting for buses? No. We talked about all the good things happening in Sunday school, where she's worked in some capacity for 67 years. Her jobs have varied according to need. Some were visible and important, others were quiet and unseen. Quit? Never.

What a precious model for others. In fact, what a precious model for me.

"Lord, may I grow old physically without letting my commitment to You and Your work grow old. You may change the contribution You want me to make, but keep me able to contribute."

Living like this means that my attitudes must stay healthy. Like a child on Christmas morning, I want to keep reaching for what's coming next.

"Please, Lord, don't ever let a disease of attitude keep me from this joy."

I want to be known for seeing sunshine, even on a gloomy day. Do you?

## For Your Study

1.  Draw a picture of a woman with a positive attitude (stick figures are fine). Explain the picture. Why have you included the various elements?

2.  Have your ever "dressed for depression or failure?" Draw a picture of that experience.

3.  Agree/disagree: A believer's attitude depends on her relationship with God.

4.  The five potential attitude diseases are: indifference, indecision, doubt, worry and overcaution. To which are you most susceptible?
> Pinpoint, if you can, what causes it to flare up.
> How will you build immunity?

5.  How can you help another believer who is coming down with an attitude disease?

Footnotes:
1.  Charles R. Swindoll, *Strengthening Your Grip* (Waco, Tex., Word Books, 1983), p.207.
2.  Webster, s.v. attitude.
3.  Ted W. Engstrom, *The Pursuit of Excellence* (Grand Rapids, Mich.: Zondervan Publishing House, 1982), p.52.

# 6
# *Facing The Report Card*

A missionary couple comes home for their first furlough. They are barely beginning to speak the language. Their child has not adjusted well to the field. Only a small Bible study is going in the area where they were assigned. Can they claim success?

The pastor's annual report reflects conflict within the church. Ministering to hurting people takes most of his time. Sunday school attendance is up. The only baptisms have been children of church families. Is this success?

A committed believer has given up church duties because of stress at home. She attends Sunday morning church services and tithes regularly. She worships and prays every day. Is this success?

What is success? We readily admit that God doesn't intend for us to fail, but how do we know when we succeed? And is it possible to succeed on earth?

Webster's dictionary says that success is "attaining one's desired end."[1] But for believers this isn't good enough. Our desired end isn't the goal. We want God's approval. Yet, what does God's approval look like when it comes?

Some Christians equate success with things going well. Wealth, good health, emotional positiveness and children who behave are evidences of success. Unsolved problems and unmet needs indicate God's disapproval. They say, "If I live a holy life, I can tell God what I want and expect Him to provide it. Therefore, success is measured by the amount of world's goods I own and whether or not things are going my way."

Other Christians say it's ungodly to talk about success at all. God alone judges. Trying to measure results is a sinful exercise that feeds the ego. There's a very real danger of receiving your reward here on earth instead of in heaven.

## The Prairie Chicken's Mistake

Somewhere between these extremes are the rest of us. We don't exactly expect success to come in the form of a bank account. On the other hand, we aren't sure we should ever experience lengthy periods of difficulty either. In our confusion, the tendency is to allow other humans to tell us what we should be.

An American Indian tells about a brave who found an eagle's egg and put it into the nest of a prairie chicken. The eaglet hatched with the brood of chicks and grew up with them. All his life, the changeling eagle, thinking he was a prairie chicken, did what the prairie chickens did. He scratched in the dirt for seeds and insects to eat. He clucked and cackled. And he flew in a brief thrashing of wings and flurry of feathers no more than a few feet off the ground. After all, that's how prairie chickens were supposed to fly.

Years passed. And the changeling eagle grew very old. One day, he saw a magnificent bird far above him in the cloudless sky. Hanging with graceful majesty on the powerful wind currents, it soared with scarcely a beat of its strong golden wings.

"What a beautiful bird," said the eagle to his neighbor. "What is it?"

"That's an eagle—the chief of birds," the neighbor clucked. "But don't give it a second thought. You could never be like him."

So the eagle never gave it another thought and died thinking it was a prairie chicken. [2]

"What a tragedy," writes the author. "Built to soar into the heavens, but conditioned to stay earthbound...designed to be among the most awesome of all fowl, instead he believed his neighbor's counsel: 'Hey, you're only a prairie chicken. Come on, let's go find some insects' "[3]

How can you avoid that prairie chicken's mistake? By knowing who you are and acting like who you are. For a Christian that means recognizing that you are God's child and acting like God's child.

## Knowing Who You Are

One part of Robert Schuller's teaching interests me. He says that the greatest tragedy in Adam and Eve's sin was their loss of self-esteem. Think of women you know who are drifting through life. Homemaker or career woman, their lives are spent putting one foot ahead of the next, doing what needs to be done. In the extreme, such women are suicidal. More often than not, they live with mediocrity.

If only they knew their status as God's children. The issue is not salvation. What's missing is recognition of their part in the purpose and plan of Holy God.

Women who connect with the fact that they're part of God's plan are exciting. They're like a radiant young woman I heard recently singing, "Only Jesus Can Satisfy a Soul." Her talent had always been there, her radiance had not. Knowing the Lord since childhood had not kept her from losing an awareness of what God could mean in her life. Like losing the instructions to a piece of needlework, she found her life in so many pieces of tangled thread. Striving for material things, she became lonely and unfulfilled.

Finally, when all of life's promises seemed broken, she turned back to God. What a homecoming! The exhilaration of her salvation flooded her world. Radiantly she sings now, "Only Jesus Can Satisfy a Soul." Now she knows with certainty that she is God's child. And she is letting her life be directed according to His plan.

## Acting Like Who You Are

Life is filled with choices. Knowing I am God's child doesn't mean I will choose to let this affect how I live. "Coming" and "following" are specific commands in Scripture. Foster parents know the need for children to follow. One child may enter their home delighted by his new-found security and provision. But will he follow the house rules? How stifling and old-fashioned. As for helping maintain the home by cleaning his room or doing kitchen duty, this interferes with his freedom.

Such rules as "Home by midnight," "Tell us where you'll be," "No smoking or drinking," are for the natural-born children. Following the family's lifestyle never happens for this child. Eventually the relationship fails, all because of the child's choice. He refused to follow.

Other children may enter foster homes determined to live like the people who've accepted them. Ethnic and cultural uniqueness are unimportant. They view their personhood as enhanced by this new way to live. They are glad to choose to follow.

## We Have Choices

When we enter God's family, we have the same choice—to follow, or go our way. Our potential for success lies in our willingness to follow His pattern for living. When we choose to follow, our personhood is enhanced, not stifled by God's ways.

The formula seems simple: Knowing who you are + acting like who you are = success. Or: God's child who acts like God's child will be successful.

If this is so, then why do so few claim success? Defining success is part of the difficulty. But David Watson suggests a number of other reasons: a lack of personal commitment, unconfessed sin, complacency, unbelief and fear.[4]

1. *A lack of personal commitment.*

One night a week our local newspaper lists the possibilities for involvement in our community. Read and drool. You can volunteer at the hospital, take a class in quilting, join a health club (half price), go to a concert, take a bus trip, try the new Greek restaurant. You want to do them all, along with all the other opportunities mentioned at church, over the radio and by friends.

One trend of the 1980s is the multiplicity of choices. The end of the decade will see this trend continuing and growing. Yet each choice brings a claim on your time and resources.

God's people can and should be a part of many of these activities. Being the salt of the earth demands it. Enriched lives, positive relationships and opportunities to witness come from such involvement. However, sometimes we must say no to many of these opportunities because we have a commitment to God's best for us. The choices we face are not between good vs. bad. But our success depends on our being faithful to what's important to God.

2. *Unconfessed sin.*

One of our boys came running into the house after school one day so excited he almost knocked me over. His pockets were full of gumballs.

"Where did you get those?" I asked.

"The machine's broken at the gas station. Here, take these! I'm going back for more," he said quickly, shoving his loot towards me.

"Wait!" I cried, pulling him back. "Honey, that's stealing."

"Oh, Mom, everybody's doing it. The guy at the gas station doesn't care."

Try as I might, I couldn't convince him that "everybody's doing it" doesn't make it right. We counted the gumballs and he paid for them out of his allowance only because I exerted parental authority. On that day, knowing he was God's child had nothing to do with how he acted.

Sin confuses. Mental processes are muddied by it. Boundaries between what we can and cannot do become mixed. A respectable way of describing our sin covers it. Gossip hides as concern. Elevation of self is called doing a better job for God. Absence from worship is deemed a necessity because of too many Christian projects during the week. This bent toward rationalization points to our constant need to stay close to God and His Word.

Regardless of its level or importance, seeing our sin requires confessing it and running away from it. As Hebrews 12 says, "Strip it off, throw it aside and run as fast as you can in the opposite direction." You don't have time to test your resistance to temptation. Sin causes hollow ministry, a lack of success.

3. *Complacency*

Life is good. Don't be so bothered with those church things. Relax. God loves you. This is a nice rut. Let's put up our mailbox.

One day follows another. Are they perfect? No, but they're routinely comfortable. No unsettling new adjustments to make.

Gradually the desire to reach beyond our routine and into God's plans diminishes and eventually is gone.

Complacency is a sign of spiritual sickness just as lack of hunger for food is a sign of physical sickness. Watson describes the way back, beginning with studying the Beatitudes:

"I began to see how spiritually poor I really was...in my heart I knew it, though I had often tried to cover it up with active Christian ministry....I became genuinely concerned at my lack of love for Jesus, my low level of faith, my disobedience in various areas of my life....I saw myself at the foot of the cross, silently weeping for my spiritual poverty. Then I became very hungry...and thirsty for righteousness."[5]

Complacency cannot exist when we know who are are and have a desire to live for God.

4. *Unbelief.*

Expectations, our own and those of others, can keep us from believing that God wants to use us. As I've said, I'm a pastor's wife. And you wouldn't believe the baggage I brought with me to this role. One bundle of concern I carried was my lack of musical talent. Churches expect the pastor's wife to have musical ability, or so I thought. Oh, dear.

Music was a part of my childhood. Being southerners, Mom and Dad both played stringed instruments. Company coming meant guitars, banjos, mandolins, etc. The men tuned up while the women put the food on. After eating, everyone played and sang and visited. Well, not everyone. There was myself.

If I followed Dad's timing, I could fill in on piano. But my playing was just that, a fill-in. Sing? Only hesitantly in especially noisy groups. My inability could easily have kept me from believing God could use me.

Thankfully, I knew about the Parable of the Talents. God gives each of us at least one talent. Even though the distribution may seem arbitrary and uneven, each of us is responsible in some area of God's work. That's God's expectation. He looks for success in our assigned areas.

Not only do our expectations trap us, but changing circumstances can cause us to believe we are no longer useable. During my boys' teen years, I sighed to a friend that I wished things would get back to normal. Home felt like a bus station. Necessities barely got done, let alone the want-to's. I was looking forward to things being as they had been.

Then my friend woke me up. "Roberta, this *is* normal. You're not living in those years anymore. You never will again."

Thank You, Lord, for honest friends. I had been looking for a set of circumstances to confirm that God could use me. When the boys had been small, I could get the house in order early in the day and have time to do lots of church work. Those days were gone. Life had turned a corner, and God had too. I had allowed myself to be left behind.

Lord, help us turn the corners with You. Teach us to believe that our potential for success is in the present tense.

The teen years for my boys meant more ministry to family than to the church. How beautiful. How important.

5. *Fear.*

"But how? When? Why?" Sounding more like reporters than followers of God, we quiz Him before taking His lead. Our anxiety hits a peak when some detail is missing. Like Winnie Pooh Bear's friend Piglet, we tend to go through life walking slightly behind God, wanting lots of assurance before stepping out.

But think and rejoice! You are being led by God Himself. A Holy Spirit specialty is to train ministers. He won't throw you in over your head, beyond your ability, before your time. He will never leave you alone in ministry. Be it cookie baking, retreat speaking, playground directing, preaching—before He calls, He knows you are ready. He only calls to the level where you can succeed.

"Wouldn't it be fun to organize an exercise group at church," you daydream. "We could have a short Bible study afterward. I have that exercise record we used at the other church. Judy's been talking about a new book on servanthood. Oh, never mind. I'm not sure I should get involved."

Several days pass. You're doing dishes and the phone rings.

"Hello, the committee is meeting and we were wondering if you would put together an exercise group this fall. Judy says she'd love to do a Bible study to go with it. It would make a great Thursday night package."

How can you say no? You're on a level where you're capable. You've already daydreamed some of the details. No need to fear. Say yes. Success is just around the corner.

Scripture teaches that believers are accountable for following God's leading. Our success is important to Him. Someday He will ask us about the doors He opened, the talents He gave.

Ted Engstrom says: "None of us will be judged on the perfection index....The questions to each of us will be: Did you make the most of your talents? Did you work toward developing your potential? Did you choose excellence, or did you coast?[6]

When the faithful servant in the Parable of the Talents stood before the Him, the Lord said: "Well done, thou good and faithful servant; thou hast been faithful over a few things, I will make thee ruler over many things. Enter thou into the joy of thy Lord."

Good?

Faithful?

Enter into the joy of the Lord?

So *that's* how God measures success!

Isn't it time you rolled up your sleeves and got to work? Isn't it time to know who you are—God's child—and to begin acting that way in your world?

## For Your Study

1.   What factors usually influence your opinion about whether or not you're succeeding in a specific ministry? Examples:
        other people's opinions
        number of people on which it has an impact
        meeting established goals
        good planning/strategy
        knowledge you've done your best
        What other examples can you think of?

2.   Why do you feel that the words "good and faithful" were used to commend the successful servant in the Parable of the Talents? How might these words relate to the definition of success given in this chapter: Success is knowing you are God's child acting like God's child.

3.   In what way has knowing you are God's child had an impact on your ability to start ministry, continue ministry and accept changes in ministry.

4.   How does acting like God's child have an impact on your ministry?

Footnotes:

1.   Webster, s.v. success.
2.   Engstrom, *The Pursuit of Excellence,* pp.15-16.
3.   Ibid, p.16.
4.   David Watson, *Called and Committed* (Wheaton, Ill.: Harold Shaw Publishers, 1982), pp.78-80).
5.   Ibid, p.79.
6.   Engstrom, pp.32-33.